MUSICIANS INSTITUTE ™

ESSENTIAL CONCEPTS

JAZZ
Drumm

T0085317

How to Apply Your Vocabulary to the Drum Kit in a Musical Fashion

by DONNY GRUENDLER

Edited by Rick Mattingly

All music composed by
Donny Gruendler

All music recorded by
Donny Gruendler and Jace McDonald at Inc. Studios

Audio mixing and mastering
Donny Gruendler

Illustrations
Donny Gruendler

Photos of Author
Jon Hastings, Paper Submarine

Instructional Photos
Jace McDonald

Cover Photo
Jon Hastings for Paper Submarine

Additional Musicians
Justin Apergis: Upright Bass
Travis Newlon: Guitar
Ron Dziubla: Tenor Saxophone
Lee Thornburg: Trumpet

This book is dedicated to the memory of
Chuck Silverman and Sandy Feldstein

To access audio visit:
www.halleonard.com/mylibrary

Enter Code
8656-6516-6242-0351

ISBN 978-1-4803-9488-9

HAL•LEONARD®
CORPORATION
7777 W. BLUEMOUND RD. P.O. BOX 13819 MILWAUKEE, WI 53213

In Australia Contact:
Hal Leonard Australia Pty. Ltd.
4 Lentara Court
Cheltenham, Victoria, 3192 Australia
Email: ausadmin@halleonard.com.au

Visit Hal Leonard Online at
www.halleonard.com

Acknowledgements

My family and friends

Thanks to my incredible wife, Hope, for her love, support, and friendship; my son, DeeGee, for his immense joy and inspiration; my Gram for all of her support over the years; Bob Terry for his friendship, support, and countless hours of advice; John and Esther Good for their love, friendship, and huge meals; Denny Freeman for allowing me to experiment on a countless number of gigs; The Church of Monday Night Football; *Mr. Inspiration* Casey Scheuerell; Steve Houghton; the percussion staff at Berklee College of Music; all my colleagues at Musicians Institute; Mike Dawson; Theseus Montgomery; Padron Maduro 3k; Reginald Bloomfield; Jace McDonald; Jesse Stern; Kirk Fletcher; Bobby Tsukamoto; Rick Holmstrom; MPCs; 6-lug; Charlie Sputnik; Art Bleek; Piano Black lacquer; Little-Airplane-Bottles-O-S; Mike Hoff for his immense support (so early on in my career); Joe Bergamini for always having my back; Sandy Feldstein (I miss you every day); Dr. Evgeny Tsimerinov; Russ Miller; Rhett Frazier; Rob Wallis; Stewart Jean; John "J.R." Robinson; Jon Clayden for always challenging me to deliver; Coko Johnson; Derek Jones; Chuck Silverman (we had so many great times together); Dee-Troyt; Versa Manos for my "doctorate"; Sara Tuchmayer (you're a life saver); Christian Lundberg; Joe Tamel, a.k.a. "tweaks," for helping with *everything*; Hank Greenburg; Al Kaline; Megatron; and everyone who has helped, inspired, or put up with me through the years. My composing, programming, and drumming are dedicated to the memory of my parents, Donald and Marilla Gruendler.

The fine companies that have supported me through the years

Vic Firth Inc.: Joe Testa, Ben Davies, Neil Larrivee, Christian Lyman, and Mark Wessels for believing in (and supporting) me for all these years; **Yamaha Corporation of America:** John Wittman, Athan Billas, Dave Jewel, Greg Crane, Steve Fisher, Mike Sutton, and Daryl Anderson for the toughest (and best sounding) drums I have ever played; **Yamaha DTX:** *My main man* Bob Terry; **Paiste America Inc.:** Kelly Paiste, Andrew Shreve, Tim Shahady, and Arturo Gil for all their time, support and wonderfully articulate cymbals; **Remo Inc.:** Bruce Jacoby for his support and friendship; **Steinberg North America:** Brian McGovern and Robert Sermeño; **EV microphones:** Guy Low; **Ableton:** Dave Hillel, Cole Goughary, and Dennis DeSantis; **Modern Drummer:** Mike Dawson, Bob Berenson, Adam Budofsky, Billy Amendola, and Tracey Kearns for always including me in their magazine and initiatives; **Gator Cases:** Brian Larsen; **Hal Leonard Publishing:** Jeff Schroedl, Rick Mattingly, Jackie Muth, and the entire HL staff for making this project a reality.

About the Author

Donny Gruendler was born and raised in the diverse musical surroundings of Detroit, Michigan. As a result, he grew up alongside an unusually broad range of influences including soul, funk, pop, hip-hop, traditional swing, hard bop, techno, house, and blues.

At age twenty, Gruendler graduated from Berklee College of Music with a Bachelor of Music Degree. At age 21, he earned his Master of Music Degree from Wayne State University in Detroit, Michigan. Now living in Los Angeles, Gruendler has performed, programmed, toured, and recorded behind such artists as Kenny Burrell, John Medeski, D.J. Logic, the Funk Brothers, D.J A-Ski (Unique 74), Rick Holmstrom, and Kirk Fletcher. He has composed and/or played on jingles for Axe Body Spray, RE/MAX on the Boulevard, and NPR. His select film/TV credits include *Last Holiday*, *Father of Invention*, and the Showtime feature *Chicago Overcoat*. Donny is also a noted producer under the pseudonym Inc and one half of the funky-jazz-soul-electro duo Rhett Frazier Inc. *Okayplayer* describes their productions as "cosmic brilliance delivered via a well-stirred pot of soul, jazz, rock, funk, and gospel."

In the education realm, Gruendler is Vice President of Academic Affairs at Musicians Institute in Hollywood, California, and he is also a member of the *Modern Drummer* education team and a frequent columnist for the magazine. Donny has also released many instructional books, DVDs and online content under his own name. For more information, please visit www.donnygruendler.com

Table of Contents

Overview

Explanation

This text is designed to help today's rock, pop, and R&B drummer quickly (and efficiently) learn the jazz idiom. It is an inclusive and in-depth study of how to authentically perform alongside a rhythm section—within jazz's popular styles and forms. Not only does this package include a set of detailed charts, but each composition also focuses on a particular musical form, drumset sound, solo concept, and comping approach. Genre-relevant drumset-based rudimental voicings and simple brush patterns will also be presented. Upon completing this study, readers will be able to function within a jazz ensemble (and sound like they belong there).

Basic musical assumptions

It is assumed that anyone reading this material has a basic knowledge of note and rest values, including eighth notes, eighth-note triplets, and quarter-note triplets, as well as drumset reading, basic chart reading, and some level of coordinated independence. However, if you need any additional information on basic drum technique or reading, there are many fine books available from Hal Leonard that can aid you in your studies.

What if you cannot read music?

I certainly suggest that you find a reputable drum instructor in your area and take some lessons to remedy the situation. However, I do realize that many who are reading this book do not have the resources to take lessons or do not have the time to attend those lessons. Therefore, you will have to intensify your conceptual and listening skills. This can be accomplished by listening to the demonstration media and by seeking out songs from within the transcription units. Many of these titles are readily available on YouTube, iTunes, Beats Music, or Spotify.

Media

Each chapter contains demonstration and play-along media. These include drumset demonstrations, bass lines, and full tunes.

Format: Order of study

Unlike many instructional books, the topics presented in this book are not based on a series of coordination or independence exercises. Rather, each unit (and corresponding exercise) presents genre relevant material alongside a myriad of rhythmic options, which are meant to unlock your own creativity—alongside a *real* tune. Thus, you will be able to immediately apply these new items to songs—i.e., use them in a musical fashion. In addition, each unit presents information in the following order:

- **Notation, Structure, and Form:** An in-depth discussion of each tune's form, feel(s), and various chart elements.
- **Performance Notes:** Detailed performance instructions, which include appropriate comping patterns, setups, and drumset sounds.
- **Play-Alongs:** The culmination of each unit—a play-along track (recorded by a real jazz ensemble).

Furthermore, some units also contain:

- **Rudimental solo studies:** Jazz rudimental voicings and their application (as made popular by many classic jazz drumming innovators).
- **Transcriptions:** These select sections present famous transcriptions, which will be applied to play-along tunes.

Notation key

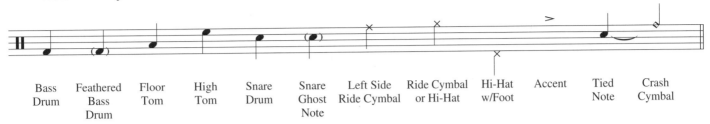

| Bass Drum | Feathered Bass Drum | Floor Tom | High Tom | Snare Drum | Snare Ghost Note | Left Side Ride Cymbal | Ride Cymbal or Hi-Hat | Hi-Hat w/Foot | Accent | Tied Note | Crash Cymbal |

Double barline: A double barline signifies the end of a section or musical phrase.

Final barline: A final barline marks the end of a composition.

Start repeat sign/End repeat sign: Repeat signs indicate that a certain musical phrase will be repeated.

| Double Bar Line | Final Bar Line | Start Repeat | End Repeat |

Time slashes: Time slashes not only mark the beats of a measure, but they also indicate that a drummer plays "time" (i.e., grooves) as well.

Repeat previous bar: A sign indicating to repeat the previous measure.

Multiple bar repeat: A sign indicating that you must repeat a certain number of bars. There usually is a number above the symbol signifying the exact number of bars to be repeated.

| Time Slashes | Fill Markers | Repeat Previous Bar | Multiple-Bar Repeat |

Rehearsal letters: These are symbols used to identify certain sections within a chart. In addition, each letter usually represents a new idea, groove, and melodic motif. These can also be marked as sections, such as Intro or Riff.

D.C. (*da capo*): Return to the beginning of the chart.

D.C. al Fine: Again, D.C. signifies that you must return to the beginning of the chart. *Fine* is a musical term for "end." Thus, you will return to the beginning of the chart (D.C.) and end when you see the term "Fine."

QR codes

Throughout the book, you will see small graphics like the one to the left. It is a QR code, which is a two-dimensional graphic that has a web address embedded within it. These codes will enable you to access the various innovators' biographies online from your smart phone or tablet device. You can download free QR readers from both the Apple app store and Google Play.

The innovators

While working through this book, you will notice that each chapter begins with a sketch of, and QR link to, an influential jazz drumset artist. Please take a moment to investigate these artists. Not only will these help you to relate to the music on an intellectual (and emotional) level, but it will also aid you in fully understanding jazz drumming as an art form.

More than drumming: It's time to talk about music

It is extremely important that you do not think "drumistically" when working through each unit, concept, or exercise. **This book is not only about drumming; it is also about *music*.** Musical sophistication, groove, feel, consistency, and comfort level take time to master. If you rush through the material and do not follow the proper methodologies—or if you just read through each section of this text—you will be defeating the purpose of your study.

Track 1

Introduction and Demo Tune

This full demo tune utilizes many of the timekeeping clichés, drumset sounds, and solo concepts presented in this book. As such, I hope it inspires you to get to work!

Unit One: 12-Bar Blues

1

Scan for bio.

Kenny Clark

Description

In this unit, you will learn to interpret a lead sheet, comp the melody, and "tag" the ending within a 12-bar blues form. The balance of jazz drum sound will also be presented.

Upon completion of this unit, you should be able to:
- Understand, interpret, and play a 12-bar-blues lead sheet
- Comp a 12-bar melody with long and short notes
- Tag and command an ending with a band
- Begin to develop a stylistically correct drum sound

Chapter 1: Lead Sheet Interpretation

The blues is one of America's greatest musical treasures—a roots-music form that evolved from African-American work songs, field hollers, spirituals, and country string ballads more than a century ago. The blues is the foundation of virtually every major form of American music born in the 20th century, including jazz, rhythm & blues, rock and roll, and hip-hop. This unit's chart will focus on a jazz interpretation of the blues, which allows us to focus on the jazz ride cymbal pattern and select kick and snare comping within the "Head" (melody).

Lead Sheet

A lead sheet is a sketch of a composition, and it is usually provided to a small ensemble. Unlike a full-blown chart, which contains every piece of musical information, a lead sheet is a modest chart that only specifies a song's melody, chord structure, form, and some basic information about the style (e.g., "medium swing"). Each player (within the group) is expected to be proficient on his or her instrument and know how to read a lead sheet. Together, these attributes help the players create the appropriate musical parts on their instruments.

 # Mr. J.D.

Track 2

Example 1.1

Drumset Interpretation

Lead sheets do not contain "beats." The drummer must create the appropriate feel (and corresponding sound) based on the style indicated (ballad, 2-feel, Latin, shuffle, etc.). Since a lead sheet is not a drum chart, it is neither necessary nor desirable for the drummer to play every figure (or rhythm) that is written within the music. You must be much more selective when choosing which figures to play. *Playing time through the majority of the figures and marking the form should be the norm.* Fills and fill markers are not written in either. As a result, it is also up to the drummer when (and if) a transition fill is necessary. Therefore, your own personal interpretation and creativity are vital in shaping the music.

12-Bar Blues

The most common musical form of blues is the 12-bar blues. The term "12-bar" refers to the number of measures, or musical bars, used to express the theme of a typical blues song. A 12-bar blues is divided into three four-bar segments. A standard blues progression typically features three chords based on the first (written as I), fourth (IV), and fifth (V) notes of an eight-note scale. In this case, I have substituted two of the major chords in a 12-bar blues with the parallel minor chords to create a minor blues. Therefore, the i (Cmi7) chord dominates the first four bars; the iv (Fmi7) chord appears in the second four bars, and the V dominant (G7) chord is played in the third four bars. (The G7 creates a "turnaround" back to the Cmi7/I chord). For example:

Mr. J.D.

Example 1.2

"Open Form": The 12-bar blues is considered an open form. This means that the song (or chart) is played (and subsequently repeated) in 12-bar increments without a specifically stated form. Therefore, the 12-bar form (chart) will be performed in 12-bar increments (12-24-36-48-60-72 bars).

Both major and minor key blues tunes utilize two additional terms that modify the form: (1) Head and (2) Chorus. Let's take a look at each (as well as how the drums address these sections) in greater detail.

The Head

The term "Head" is most often used in jazz or blues contexts, and it refers to the thematic melody within a song's form. This melody is usually played at the beginning and at the end of a song's performance. Thus, if a bandleader requests one Head (in a 12-bar form), the band would play through twelve bars of the melody, as shown in example 1.2.

Note: Jazz and blues musicians also often give each other the "head" or "top" cue by patting their hand on top of their head, which is usually meant to make sure everybody "goes back to the melody" the next time the "top of the form" comes around.

A Chorus

Unlike a pop music chorus, which refers to the "hook" of a song, a jazz or blues chorus is a term that is slang for "one time through the form."

Thus, when bandleaders say they want to play one chorus of guitar solo (in a 12-bar blues form), they are requesting 12 bars of guitar solo through the chords of the song (i.e., one 12-bar blues). For example:

Mr. J.D.

Track 3

Example 1.3

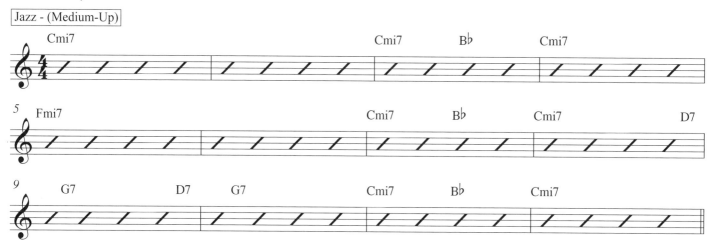

Chapter 2: Timekeeping and Comping

Comping is short for "accompanying," and it is how the rhythm-section instruments—such as piano, guitar, and drums—support both the head (melody) and the soloist (choruses of solo). Let's take a look at musical comping within the structure of this lead sheet's specific melody and head.

Important: Comping is NOT "complex independence patterns to play beneath the ride cymbal." Nor is it a place to display your thousand variations of beat displacements.

Comping the Head

During the head, the drums should support the melody line by accompanying and accentuating notes within each phrase. These are articulated by note duration, and they can be accented by either the snare drum or bass drum. The ride cymbal pattern and hi-hat are frequently unchanged. Yet, you can also change the ride cymbal to accentuate the longer notes within a head's melody, too. For this reason, it is very important to develop the proper independence to either keep the ride and hi-hat going, or "vary" them while playing various accents with the snare and/or bass drum.

Ride Cymbal Unchanged Let's take a look at example 1.4 (bars 1–4 from the head). You will notice that the bass drum and snare drum comp with the written melody, and the ride cymbal and hi-hat remain unchanged:

Example 1.4

Ride Cymbal Variation—Accentuating the Long Notes: In example 1.5, taken from the head, you will notice that the bass drum and snare drum still comp with the written guitar melody. However, each long note is now played with a shouldered ride accent (marked by tied cymbal notes), which subsequently changes the ride cymbal pattern:

Example 1.5

So how can you develop the proper independence and "know-how" to musically comp the head? Some common rules are as follows:

Short notes (eighth note) = short sounds—snare drum (alone) or bass drum (alone).

Long notes (tied eighth note, quarter, or dotted-quarter)—snare drum or bass drum reinforced with a shouldered ride cymbal or crash cymbal.

Isolating Each Section of the 12-Bar Head

This medium-up tempo 12-bar blues jazz lead sheet is comprised of three four-bar phrases. Within each phrase the melodies are similar in bars 2, 6, and 10—and again in bars 3, 7, and 11. There is also a tag/turnaround in bars 9–12. Let's go through each unique melodic phrase individually and discuss how to play, navigate, and interpret them on the drumset.

Example 1.6

Bars 2, 6, and 10

In bars 2, 6, and 10 there are two long notes, the dotted-quarter on beat 1 and the quarter note on the "&" of beat 3. There are also three short notes on the "&" of beat 2, beat 3, and the "&" of beat 4:

Example 1.7

With these ideas in mind, some acceptable comping options are:

Example 1.8

14

Bars 2, 6, and 10: Preliminary Exercises and Performance Suggestions

In order to develop the musical "know how" and independence to play these measures, you should work through all three sections: The preliminary exercises (with the ride cymbal unchanged) and Cymbal Variations 1 and 2, which vary the jazz ride pattern by accentuating the long notes with a shouldered ride cymbal accent. Each exercise is played four times on the audio, and preceded by two measures of time.

 Example 1.9

Track 4

Preliminary Independence Exercises

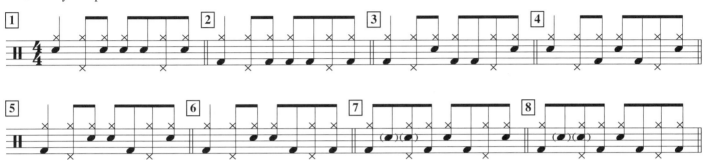

 Example 1.10

Track 5

Note Duration: Shouldering the Long Notes
Cymbal Variation 1

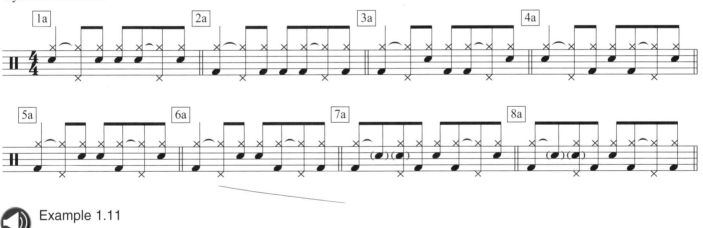

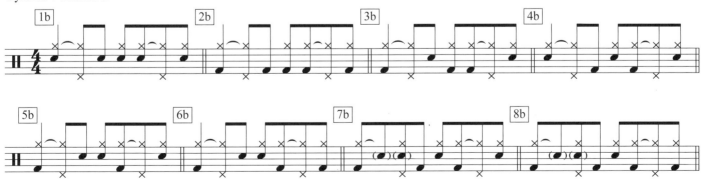

Example 1.11

Track 6

Note Duration: Shouldering the Long Notes
Cymbal Variation 2

Bars 3, 7, and 11

Only long notes are present within bars 3, 7, and 11: a half note on beat 1, a dotted-quarter note on beat 3, and a tied eighth note on the "&" of beat 4. Following the common comping suggestions from the previous pages, some acceptable comping options are:

Example 1.12

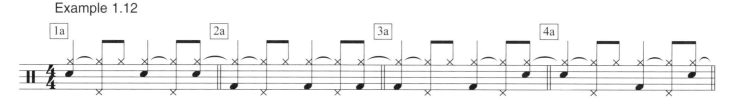

Notice that each long note is reinforced with a shouldered ride cymbal.

Bars 3, 7, and 11: Preliminary Exercises and Performance Suggestions

In order to develop the musical "know how" and independence to play these measures, you should work through all three sections: The preliminary exercises (with the ride cymbal unchanged) and Cymbal Variations 1 and 2, which vary the jazz ride pattern by accentuating the long notes with a shouldered ride cymbal accent. Each exercise is played four times on the audio, and preceded by two measures of time.

 Example 1.13

Track 7

Preliminary Independence Exercises

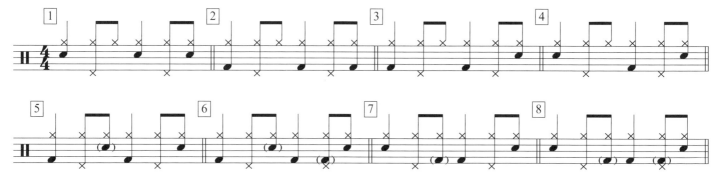

 Example 1.14

Track 8

Note Duration: Shouldering the Long Notes
Cymbal Variation 1

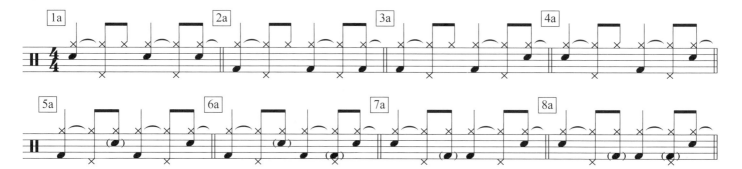

16

Track 9

Example 1.15

Note Duration: Shouldering the Long Notes
Cymbal Variation 2

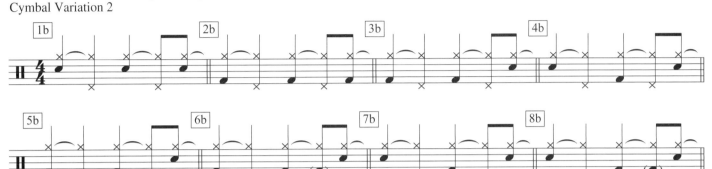

Bars 9 and 10

There are long notes on the "&"
of beat 1 in measures 9 and 10.

Following the common comping suggestions from the previous section, some musical (and acceptable) comping options are:

Example 1.16

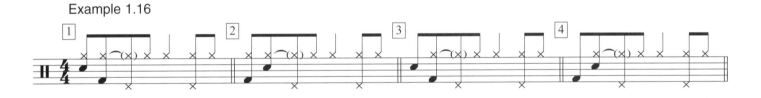

Each downbeat (of beat 1) "sets up" the melody note on the "&" of beat 1. The long notes are also reinforced with a shouldered ride cymbal.

Musical Comping: Putting It All Together

Now that you have practiced (and mastered) the individual comping patterns for each measure, I have listed one possible complete 12-bar comping example for you:

Track 10

Example 1.17

Now that you have practiced (and mastered) the individual comping patterns for each measure and the 12-bar complete comping example, write two choruses of your own comping (for the head) here:

Your Mr. JD Comping

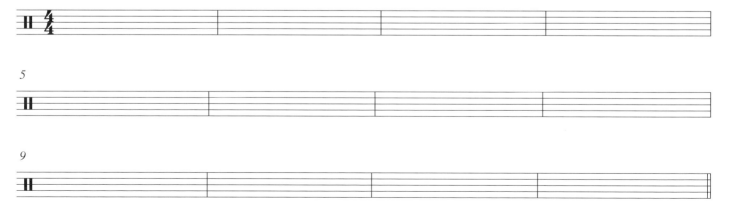

Chapter 3: Ending and Balance of Sound

As the 12-bar form (and this lead sheet) is an "open" form, it does not contain a definite ending. One common way to end the form is to "tag" the turnaround—bars 9–12.

Example 1.18

Generally it is played three times to form a definitive ending. Therefore, the last head would be played like this:

Mr. J.D.

Example 1.19

Note: Notice how the tune ends on the "&" of beat 4 in bar 11—the last note of the "tagged" ending. It is common to end a 12-bar blues in this manner, but it will not be written out on the lead sheet.

The Jazz Balance of Sound

The jazz balance of sound differs from the pop/rock balance of sound. Whereas pop/rock places the main emphasis (and strong dynamic) on the kick and snare, jazz drumming is quite the opposite. This style features the ride cymbal as the main (loudest) voice with the hi-hat a close second; the snare is just below the hi-hat, and the bass drum is the softest. Even the names of the bass drum differ in each style. Pop/rock labels the bass drum the "kick," as it is much louder than the other drumset voices. For example:

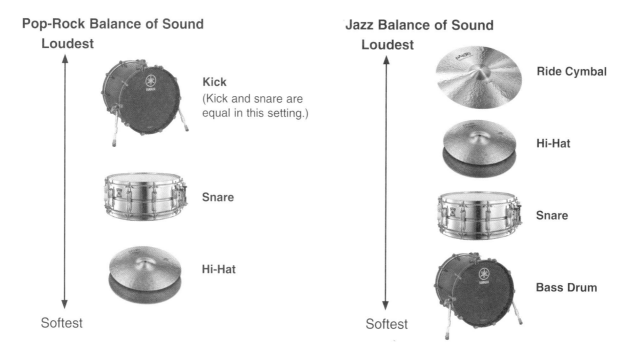

Pop-Rock Balance of Sound

Loudest

Kick
(Kick and snare are equal in this setting.)

Snare

Hi-Hat

Softest

Jazz Balance of Sound

Loudest

Ride Cymbal

Hi-Hat

Snare

Bass Drum

Softest

The Ride Cymbal: The Foundation of a Good Jazz Time Feel

The foundation of jazz drumming is the ride cymbal. The essence of a good jazz cymbal rhythm is the quarter-note pulse as shown in example 1.20. As soon as you can make that feel good, move on and add the skip note (the last note of the eighth-note triplet) to complete the full jazz-ride pattern in example 1.21.

Track 11
(Ex. 1.20-1.23)

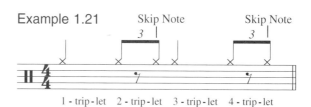

Example 1.20

Example 1.21

1 - trip - let   2 - trip - let   3 - trip - let   4 - trip - let

The normal playing area will be approximately halfway between the edge of the cymbal and the edge of the bell. This playing area will give a nice blend between definition and wash. Closer to the bell equals more definition. Closer to the edge equals more wash. It is important to note that the cymbals typically used in jazz playing are thinner than those used in rock or pop music. With these facts in mind, the ride cymbal pattern should create a large blanket of sound, which covers the entire band and connects them in one unified sound. This does not mean the cymbal should be loud, but it must be strong.

Crash Accents: "Shouldering" the Ride

In rock music, accents are "crashed" on a dedicated crash cymbal. However, jazz accents are played on the ride cymbal and they are "shouldered" with the stick. This is accomplished by using the shoulder of the stick to strike the top surface of the cymbal. Not only does this create a full washy sound, but it also helps to control the overtones of the cymbal as well as making the sound more authentic.

The Hi-Hat: The Jazz Backbeat

In straight-ahead jazz drumming, the hi-hat is typically played on counts 2 and 4 of the bar. This is very similar to pop music's backbeat function. There are at least three techniques that may be employed: (1) the rocking motion, (2) bouncing the whole leg, and (3) flat-footed. Use whichever is most comfortable to you.

Example 1.22

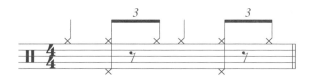

The Bass Drum: Feathering

Feathering is a common quarter-note bass drum technique, which should be felt rather than heard. This articulation should fall underneath the other drumset voices and add attack (and punch) to the jazz upright-bass walking line. **Thus, if you can *hear* the bass drum, it is too loud.**

In order to achieve this sound, use the felt side of the bass drum beater and choke up on the pedal by placing your toes just behind the chain (or strap) of the footboard. Thereafter, your beater stroke should travel backward approximately 1 to 1 1/2 inches from the head. Do not bring the beater back too far; this will result in a loud stroke and a stylistically incorrect sound.

Feathering in Time

The bass drum should strike (in perfect unison) with the ride cymbal on counts 1, 2, 3, and 4. In addition, the bass drum, hi-hat, and ride cymbal also strike together on counts 2 and 4. Therefore (and in order to avoid unwanted flamming between the voices), you should record yourself playing the following swing pattern:

Example 1.23

Marking a Song's Form

Essentially, marking a form is outlining (and drawing attention to) each different section within a song. In this unit's context, these sections are the Head and Chorus of the 12-bar minor blues. This is accomplished by employing sonic changes to the drumset by changing ride cymbals for each new section of the song. (In jazz, all cymbals are considered rides.) Therefore, the Head should have a particular cymbal/texture, and the solo Choruses should have a different cymbal/texture.

In this unit's chart, the following form, performance instructions, and cymbals will be used:

1. Head (Ride Cymbal 1)   **1**
   Comping the Head (melody)

2. Chorus 1 of Guitar Solo (Ride Cymbal 2)   **2**

3. Chorus 2 of Guitar Solo
   Comping with the soloist and feathering the bass drum

4. Head—Tagging the Turnaround 3x—(Ride Cymbal 1)   **1**

Chapter 4: The Chart and Play-Along

Mr. J.D.

Track 12 Demo
Track 13 Play-Along

Example 1.24

Form:

1. **Head** (Ride Cymbal 1): Comping the Head (melody)
2. **Chorus 1** of Guitar Solo (Ride Cymbal 2)
3. **Chorus 2** of Guitar Solo—Comping with the soloist and feathering the bass drum
4. **Head**—Tagging the Turnaround 3x (Ride Cymbal 1)

Unit Two: Turnarounds and Trading Fours

2

Scan for bio.

Billy Higgins

Description

In this unit, you will learn to tag the turnaround, incorporate flams and flam-taps into your playing, and trade fours.

Upon completion of this unit, you should be able to:

- Tag the turnaround to form an introduction (i.e. a tagged intro)
- Use flams and flam accents within your setups
- Trade 4-bar solos with other members of the band

Chapter 1: Structure – Tag the Intro

As the 12-bar form (and this lead sheet) is an "open" form, it does not contain a definite beginning or ending. In the last Unit, we added an ending to the tune by "tagging" the turnaround, i.e., bars 9–12. We played it three times to form a definitive ending. In Unit 2's chart, we are going to add the tag (bars 9–12) to the beginning of the lead sheet to form an introduction. It looks like this:

 Example 2.1

Track 14

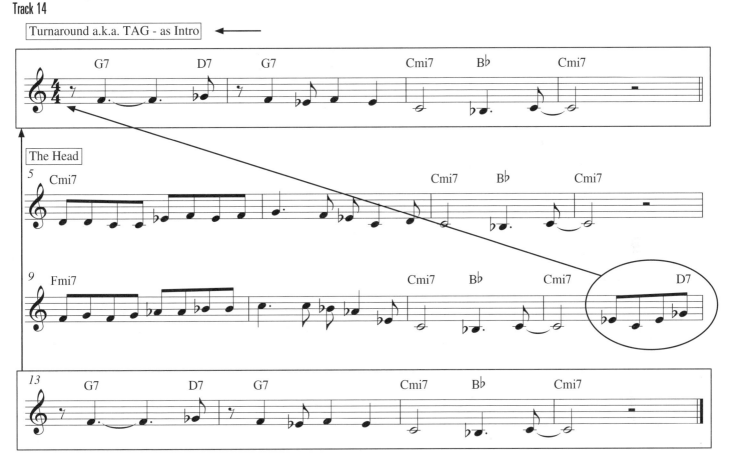

Notice how the tune begins on the "&" of beat 1 from bar 9—the first note of the "tagged" intro. It is common to begin a 12-bar blues in this manner, **but it will not be written out on the lead sheet**. During the count-in, it is also important to realize that the horns will play the last four eighth notes within bar 8—i.e. as pickup.

Drumset Intro Interpretation: Stop-Time

This newly "tagged" intro should be performed as a stop-time feel. Therefore, you should "stop playing time" and only play the rhythms that are presented within this melody. I have listed one useable and appropriate orchestration for you:

Example 2.1a

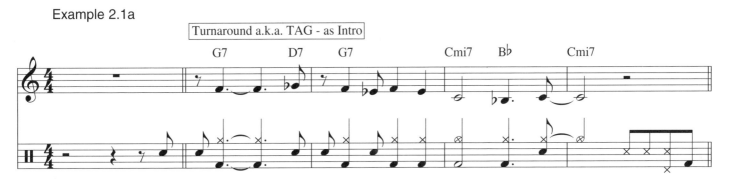

Pickup Note

The Intro begins on the "&" of beat 1. Therefore you should "set up" the upbeat figure by preceding it with a setup into the downbeat. In this case, one plausible option would be to count-in "1-2-3-4" and come in on the "&" of beat 4 as follows:

Example 2.2

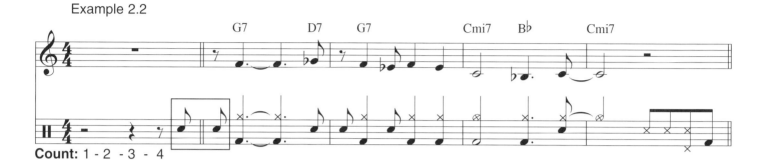

Count: 1 - 2 - 3 - 4

Pickup Fill into Letter A

Once the stop-time intro has concluded, you will need to provide a transition into the head and the jazz groove. I have listed one option for you below:

Example 2.3

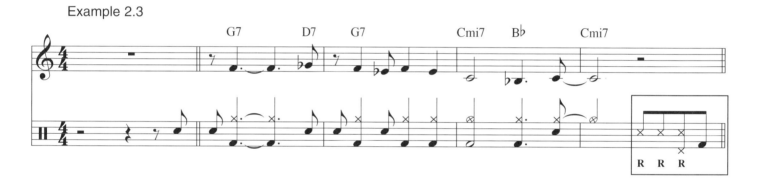

Sound Review:

Stick-Shot

In bar 4 of the tag intro, a stick-shot is used. A stick-shot is performed by placing the left stick at a 45-degree angle to the snare and pressing the bead (of the stick) into the drumhead. You should apply enough pressure to avoid a buzz sound and slightly mute the head too. The right stick then strikes the left stick and a wood-tone accent is heard. This articulation is very common in jazz solo phrases and transition fills. **(Either traditional or matched grip can be used for this technique.)**

Important Reminder: This is a lead sheet chart. Feel free to use your own creative voicings for the stop-time intro, pickup note, and pickup fill.

Chapter 2: Rudimental Basics – the Flam and Flam Tap

The flam is a combination of a stroke and a tap. The stroke is made with an arm and wrist movement, while the tap is made with the wrist (or fingers) alone. The flam is written by placing a small grace note before the large note. The purpose of the flam is to broaden the sound and tone of a drum. The sticks do not strike the head at the same time, but they must strike so close together that they will sound as one stroke.

The flam is named from the hand that plays the principal note. There are three types of flams: right flams, left flams, and alternating flams. Alternating flams are played from hand to hand, the hand that plays the stroke of the first flam stays close to the drum to be in position to play the grace note of the second (following) flam.

Example 2.4

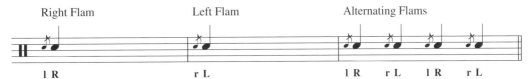

Right Flam	Left Flam	Alternating Flams
l R	r L	l R r L l R r L

The Right Flam

In order to play the right flam, hold the right stick at chin level with the stick pointing upward. Make a right stroke, and just before the stick hits the drumhead, drop the left stick onto the head. When practicing, stop both sticks approximately two inches above the drumhead.

Practice example 2.5 (below) for the development of your right flam. Keep the right hand high while playing the grace notes. After playing the fourth grace note with the left hand, make the stroke with your right hand.

Example 2.5

l l l l R   l l l l R   l l l l R   l l l l R

The Left Flam

In order to play the left flam, hold the left stick at chin level with the stick pointing upward. Make a right stroke, and just before the stick hits the drumhead, drop the left stick onto the head. When practicing, stop both sticks approximately two inches above the drumhead.

Practice example 2.6 (below) for the development of your left flam. Keep the left hand high, while playing the grace notes. After playing the fourth grace note with the right hand, make the stroke with your left hand.

Example 2.6

Alternating Flams

Start with the right stick high and the bead of the left stick 2 inches above the drumhead. Play the grace note with an upstroke (see example 2.7) and play the main stroke with a downstroke. Your sticks are now prepared (and in position) to play the next flam. When playing flams, one hand should always be raised higher than the other hand.

Example 2.7

Upstroke   Downstroke

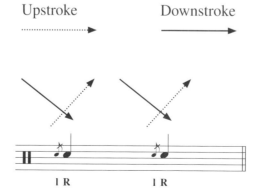

Flam Rudiment: Flam Accent No. 1

The Flam Accent No. 1 is comprised of a flam and two taps, and it is usually played in a three-note grouping in 6/8 time. The sticking is alternating except on the grace note of the flam, which is played with the same hand that plays the stroke before it.

Example 2.8

Just as in the alternating flams, the motion of this rudiment also utilizes upstokes and downstrokes to prepare for the next hand's accent and Flam.

Example 2.9

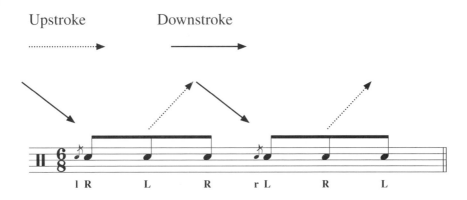

Chapter 3: The Flam and Flam Tap on the Drumset in 4/4

Jazz drumming has a strong tradition in improvisation and rudimental manipulation. Therefore, this unit's lesson features four modern interpretations of the Flam Accent No. 1. Once mastered, these concepts will be utilized within this unit's 12-bar tune while trading two-choruses of "fours."

Phrasing in 4/4: The Snare

Again, the Flam Accent No. 1 is usually played as a three-note grouping in 6/8 time.

Track 15
(Ex. 2.10–2.12)

Example 2.10

In order to use this rudiment within a 4/4 jazz context, we must phrase this three-note grouping as swing eighth notes. The hi-hat is played on beats 2 and 4. For example:

Example 2.11

By using the Flam Accent No. 1 in this manner, the rudiment becomes a three-measure phrase, with accents (or flams) on every dotted-quarter pulse. (You will notice that the fourth bar is identical to the first.) The hi-hat foot aids in developing this jazz 4/4 pulse as well. For example:

Example 2.12

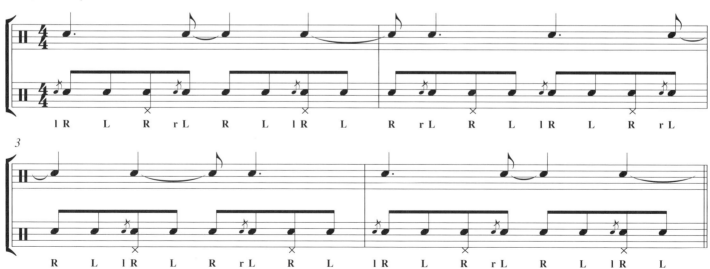

Phrasing in 4/4: Additional Jazz Drum Voicings

Obviously, there are hundreds of ways to voice this three-note rudiment on the drumkit. I have listed some of the most traditional options below. Each example is played twice on the audio.

1. Flams on the Toms

In this example, the left flam is played on the high tom and the right flam is played on the floor tom. The unaccented notes remain on the snare, and the hi-hat is played on beats 2 and 4:

**Track 16
(Ex. 2.13-2.15)** Example 2.13

2. Flams on Bass Drum and Cymbals

In this example, the left flam is played on the crash and the right flam is played on the ride cymbal **(both cymbals are reinforced with the bass drum)**. The unaccented notes remain on the snare, while the hi-hat is played on beats 2 and 4:

Example 2.14

3. Timekeeping Flam Accent

In this example, you will play the same coordination pattern from example 2.14 (the bass drum and cymbal voicing). However, in this timekeeping variation, the left hand remains on the snare, and the right hand plays on the ride cymbal in the traditional timekeeping position. Thus, the Flam Accent No. 1 will be played in this position, while reinforcing both flams with the bass drum. The hi-hat is played on beats 2 and 4:

Example 2.15

Chapter 4: Trading Fours

Trading Fours is a time-honored tradition of soloing between jazz instrumentalists and drummers. "Fours" are mini 4-bar solos, which are traded (alternated) between an instrumentalist (or group of instrumentalists) and the drummer. In the following example, the drums trade fours through two choruses of a 12-bar form. Three four-bar phrases can be traded within each chorus. The guitar begins the first chorus and the drums lead the second chorus:

Chorus 1

Example 2.16

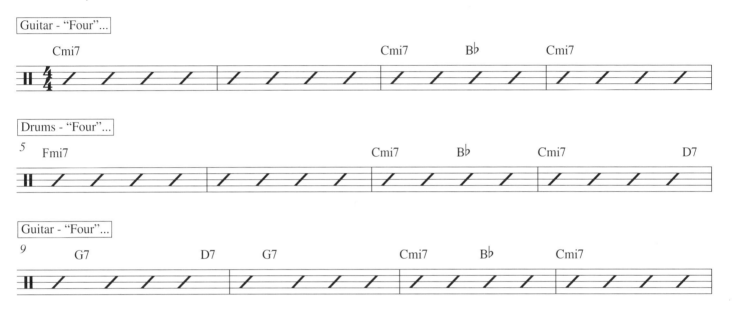

Chorus 2

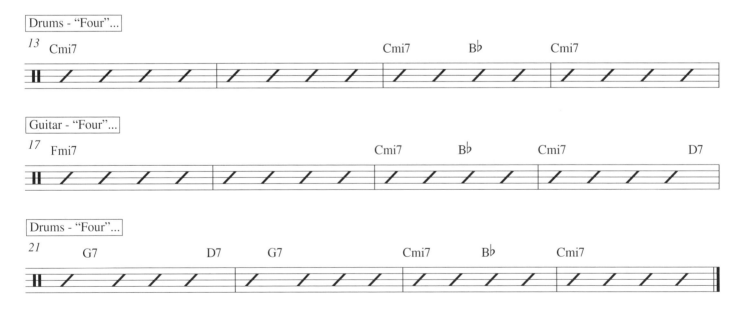

Trading Fours with the Flam Accent No. 1 Voicings

The following example uses the Flam Accent No. 1's phrases shown in examples 2.12–2.15 while trading two choruses of "fours":

 # Chorus 1

Track 17

Example 2.17

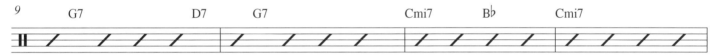

Chorus 2

Chapter 5: The Chart and Play-Along

Mr. J.D.

Track 18 Demo
Track 19 Play-Along

Example 2.18

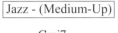

Form:
1. **Intro:** Tagging the Turnaround 1x (Stop Time)
2. **Head** (Ride Cymbal 1): Comping the Head (melody) from Unit 1
3. **Chorus 1** of Trading Fours (Ride Cymbal 2)
4. **Chorus 2** of Trading Fours
5. **Head** (Ride Cymbal 1): Comping the Head from Unit 1
6. **Outro/Ending:** Tagging the Turnaround 3x (Ride Cymbal 1)

3 Unit Three: Two-Feel and Walking-Feel

Philly Joe Jones

Scan for bio.

Description

In this unit, you will learn to play a two-feel, walking-feel, and the sock cymbal within a 12-bar blues form. A Philly Joe Jones 12-bar solo will also be presented.

Upon completion of this unit, you should be able to:
- Play a two-feel on the sock cymbal (hi-hat)
- Understand the difference between a two-feel and a walking-feel
- Understand and be able to play Philly Joe Jones solo fragments
- Play a fully notated Philly Joe Jones 12-bar drum solo

Chapter 1: Background – The Two-Feel and Sock Cymbal History

The most popular feels within jazz are the walking-feel and two-feel. Let's take a look at both in detail.

Walking-Feel

This feel is based on the quarter-note pulse, where the bass player "walks" through the chord changes. In turn, the drummer usually "feathers" the bass drum four-quarters-to-the-bar while playing time on the ride cymbal.

Example 3.1

Two-Feel

When a band member asks for a "two-feel," the bass player plays a half note-based pattern rather than "walking" a quarter-note pulse. In response, the drummer usually "feathers" the bass drum on half notes while playing time on either the hi-hat or ride cymbal.

Example 3.2

The Sock Cymbal

During the 1910s–20s, the Walberg & Auge Company invented the sock cymbal (also nicknamed the Low-Boy). This new device was the early incarnation of the modern-day hi-hat. It was originally named the sock cymbal because the cymbals were only elevated slightly off the floor, near the drummer's shoes and socks. Therefore, it could not be played with drumsticks.

Example 3.3

The Hi-Hat

In the late 1920s, many drummers wanted to play the sock cymbals with both the foot and drumsticks. Soon thereafter, Walberg & Auge, Slingerland, Ludwig, and Leedy each released sock cymbal stands with an elevated tube, which allowed the cymbals to be played with drumsticks. This new stand was named the hi-hat. By the 1930s, the hi-hat gained popularity, and the sock cymbal Low-Boy quickly went out of fashion.

Example 3.4

Chapter 2: Playing the Sock Cymbals

By today's standards, "the sock" refers to playing time on the hi-hat cymbals. Using your left foot to hold the cymbals approximately a quarter inch apart, position your left thumb on the top cymbal and your fingers on the bottom cymbal. Matched grip players: your left hand will need to be in a *fake*-traditional grip.

Example 3.5

While playing time, use your left hand (instead of your left foot) to close the cymbals on beats 2 and 4.

Correct Performance Approach

Track 20

Example 3.6

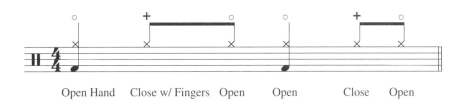

Open Hand   Close w/ Fingers   Open   Open   Close   Open

This will make the time sound even, smooth, and stylistically correct.

Incorrect Performance Approach

You should avoid a common mistake of playing two closed notes on both beats 2 and 4 like this:

Example 3.7

This will make the time sound uneven, stiff, and corny.

Two-Feel Sock Cymbal Preliminary Exercises

In order to develop the proper sock cymbal feel alongside the two-feel, I have provided some preliminary exercises below.

Track 21
(Ex. 3.8-3.11) Example 3.8

Example 3.9

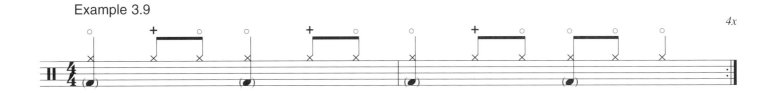

Example 3.10

Two-Feel Sock Cymbal Phrasing

Once you have mastered each two-bar phrase, try to freely move between and combine these ideas into multiple-bar phrases. I have listed one (as a example) below.

Example 3.11

Chapter 3: Philly Joe Jones and a 12-Bar Solo

In the last two units, we learned how to approach timekeeping and trading fours within a 12-bar blues form. We are now going to discuss Philly Joe Jones's drumming and his solo approach to a full chorus of drum solo within this form.

Philly Joe Jones Background

Philly Joe Jones established himself as the premier jazz drummer of the mid to late 1950s. He was a member of Miles Davis's Classic Quintet, which was one of the first small groups to feature a steady lineup. This group consisted of Miles on trumpet, pianist Red Garland, bassist Paul Chambers, tenor saxophonist John Coltrane, and Philly Joe on drums. Over the next two years, this group would record some of jazz's most revered recordings and forever be remembered as the Miles Classic Quintet. This was the band of the 1950s that was often imitated, but never duplicated.

Philly's timekeeping on the classic quintet recordings was modern, hard-hitting, polyrhythmic, form-conscious, and interactive. Jones's stylistic soloing also combined the history of jazz drumming into an all-embracing contemporary style that was at once rudimental, arrogant, thunderous, exhilarating, and impeccably musical. Some highlights from the classic Miles Davis Quintet period from 1955 to 1957 include the four famous Davis records (all recorded in one weekend) *Workin'*, *Steamin'*, *Relaxin'*, and *Cookin'*. Philly's musical legacy was largely defined within this two-year period.

Freelance Work

During this era, Jones became one of the most in-demand freelance drummers, both during and immediately after his run with the Miles Davis Quintet. One of the most famous of these recordings featured the entire Miles rhythm section of Philly Joe, Red Garland, and Paul Chambers—without Miles! It was an Art Pepper record titled *Art Pepper Meets the Rhythm Section*. Many consider this record to be a definitive source on Philly Joe's timekeeping and soloing.

"Burks Daily Work"

This unit's tune is in the style of Art Pepper's famous *Art Pepper Meets the Rhythm Section album*. This 12-bar blues employs sock cymbal timekeeping within a two-feel. Prior to the last Head, we will also perform one chorus of a 12-bar Philly Joe Jones drum solo transcription.

Example 3.12

The Head

Preliminary Solo Exercises for "Burks Daily Work"

In order to play the entire 12-bar solo correctly and comfortably, I have listed many two-bar excerpts for you below. You will notice that the stickings are included and that the hi-hat foot is notated (and closing) on beats 2 and 4.

Track 22
(Ex. 3.13-3.18) Example 3.13

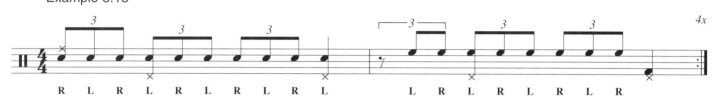

Example 3.14. The "2" above each eighth-note grouping tells you to perform those as straight eighths.

Example 3.15

Example 3.16. All sixteenth notes should be played straight.

Example 3.17. All sixteenth notes should be played straight.

Example 3.18

The Full Solo

Once you have mastered each two-bar fragment, you can begin to build and perform the full 12-bar solo. Please remember the performance notes from the preliminary exercises.

Track 23

Example 3.19

Chapter 4: The Chart and Play-Along
Burks Daily Work

Track 24 Demo
Track 25 Play-Along

Example 3.20

Form:

1. **2 Choruses** of the Head: Two-feel on the sock cymbals
2. **Chorus** of guitar solo: Ride cymbal, walking-feel
3. **Chorus** of drum solo playing the Philly Joe 12-bar solo with hi-hat on beats 2 and 4
4. **1 Chorus** of the head: Two-feel on the sock cymbals; tagging the turnaround 3x to end

Unit Four: Two-Feel on Hi-Hat: Comping

Scan for bio.

Roy Haynes

Description

In this unit, you will learn to comp the head of a 12-bar blues while playing a two-feel on the sock cymbal. Clichés for the walking-feel will also be presented.

Upon completion of this unit, you should be able to:

- Play a two-feel on the sock cymbal alongside melodic comping
- Be able to play select timekeeping clichés within the walking-feel

Chapter 1: Comping the Head in Two (on the Sock Cymbal)

Just as in Unit 1, the drums need to support the melody line by accompanying (and accentuating) select notes within each phrase of the head. Usually, these are articulated by note duration, and they can be accented by either the snare drum or bass drum. However (and it this lesson), we will be comping the head while playing a two-feel on the sock cymbal (hi-hat).

Within this feel, the hi-hat pattern is usually unchanged. For this reason, it is very important to develop the proper independence to keep the hi-hat going while playing various accents with the snare, stick-shot, and/or bass drum.

Two-Feel Comping Example

Let's take a look at example 4.1 (bars 1–4 from this unit's Head). You will notice that the bass drum and snare drum comp with the written ensemble figures, while the two-feel bass drum and hi-hat remain relatively unchanged:

Track 26
(Ex. 4.1-4.3) Example 4.1

Stick-Shot While on the Sock Cymbal

In example 4.2, measure 3 (beat 4) has a stick-shot, which sets up the ensemble figure on the "&" of beat 4. A ruff precedes this stick-shot (example 4.3) and it is played from the sock hand position (discussed on the next page).

Example 4.2

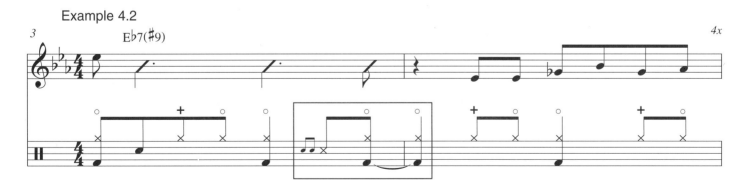

Example 4.3

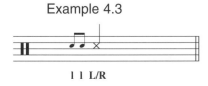

Stick-Shot: Ruff Movement and Hand Position

You must use your left foot to hold the cymbals approximately a quarter inch apart, position your left thumb on the top cymbal and your fingers on the bottom cymbal. Your left hand will be in a fake-traditional grip, with the stick tip nearly resting on the snare drum (example 4.4). While playing time, use your left hand (instead of your left foot) to close the cymbals on beats 2 and 4.

Example 4.4

Next (while still in your traditional grip), gently play a two-note light ruff on the snare, and immediately move your right hand from the time-keeping position to the stick-on-stick (stick-shot) for the third note of the ruff.

Afterward, you should return to your timekeeping position on the sock cymbal. It should look like, and be played as, follows:

Example 4.5

Example 4.6

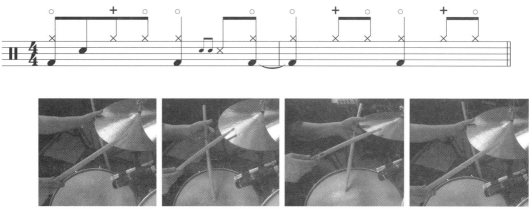

Comping: Isolating Each Section of the 12-Bar Head

This medium-tempo 12-bar blues jazz lead sheet is comprised of one main four-bar motif. Within this phrase the melodies are similar throughout the 12-bar Head. There are also two sets of ensemble figures that divide this melody.

Example 4.7

Let's go through each melodic phrase individually and discuss how to play, navigate, and interpret them.

Bars 1, 5, 9, and 11

In bars 1, 5, 9, and 11 there is a dotted-quarter on beat 3 and an eighth note on the "&" of beat 4. I have listed some possible comping orchestrations for you below.

Preliminary Exercises

Track 27

Example 4.8

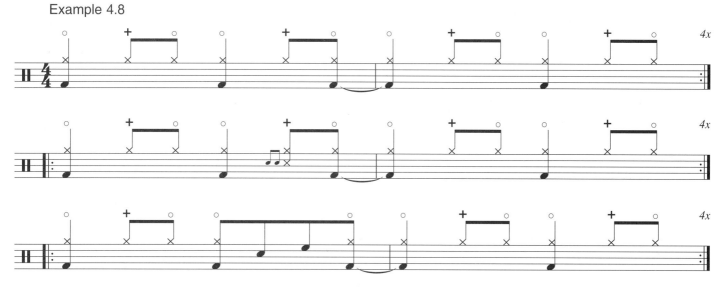

4

Bars 3, 7, and 10

In bars 3, 7, and 10 there is a dotted-quarter on the "&" of beat 1, a dotted-quarter on beat 3, and an eighth note on the "&" of beat 4. I have listed some possible comping orchestrations for you below.

Preliminary Exercises

Track 28

Example 4.9

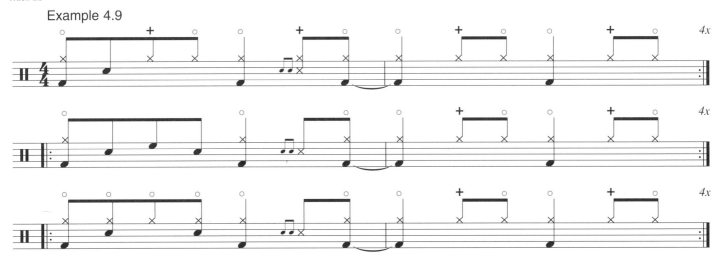

Two-Feel Sock Comping: Putting It All Together

Now that you have practiced (and mastered) the individual comping patterns for each measure, I have listed one possible complete 12-bar comping example for you:

Track 29

Example 4.10

46

Chapter 2: Walking-Feel Time Clichés

In the last three units, we have discussed how to comp (and keep time during) the head of a tune. In this chapter, we are going to begin to develop some jazz timekeeping clichés that you can utilize during another instrumentalist's chorus or solo.

Accentuate and End Phrases

Just as rock music has a standard set of groove variations and fills that connect two sections of a song, jazz has clichés. These clichés not only will help you to end phrases (which also can connect two sections of a song), but they will also help you to sound more authentic within this style. I have listed some standard one-bar and two-bar timekeeping clichés for you below.

Isolated One-Bar Phrases

Jazz timekeeping usually "anticipates" the downbeat with an accent on the "&" of any given beat. Therefore, the following four clichés "shoulder" the ride with either a bass drum or snare accent on the "&" of beat 4. (The shouldered ride is implied by a diamond notehead too.)

Track 30
(Ex. 4.11-4.13) Example 4.11

However, there are other acceptable timekeeping options. Two such clichés feature a "shouldered" accent on beat 4:

Example 4.12

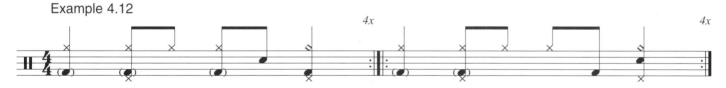

One-Bar Practice Method

Once you feel comfortable with each cliché, practice each of them within this four-bar phrase:

Example 4.13

Insert One-Bar Phrase.............

If you began with the first example in example 4.11, it would be played like this:

Example 4.14

Insert One-Bar Phrase.........................

Isolated Two-Bar Phrases

Jazz timekeeping can also feature longer phrases. Not only can you "anticipate" the downbeat with a "shouldered" accent on the "&" of any given beat; but you can also follow this accent with an immediate hi-hat accent (with the left hand) on beat 2. For example:

Track 31
(Ex. 4.15-4.16) Example 4.15

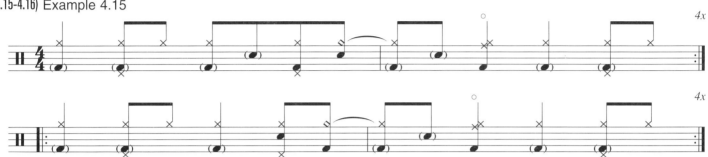

Max Roach, Philly Joe Jones, and Art Blakey made this sound (and timekeeping pattern) popular in the early 1950s.

Two-Bar Practice Method

Once you feel comfortable with each two-bar cliché, practice each of them within this four-bar phrase:

Example 4.16

If you began with the first example in example 4.15, it would be played like this:

Example 4.17

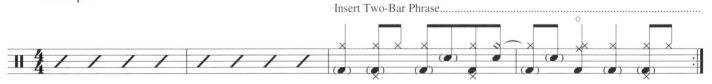

Sound Review: "Shouldering" the Ride

Jazz accents are played on the ride cymbal and they are "shouldered" with the stick. This is accomplished by using the shoulder of the stick to strike the top surface of the cymbal. Not only does this create a full, washy sound; but it also helps to control the overtones of the cymbal as well as making the sound more authentic.

Example 4.18

Chapter 3: The Chart and Play-Along

Track 32 Demo
Track 33 Play-Along

Example 4.19

Form:

1. **Two Choruses** of the Head: Two-Feel on the Sock Cymbals while comping the head
2. **Chorus** of Guitar Solo: Ride Cymbal Walking-Feel, using 1-Bar Timekeeping Clichés
3. **Chorus** of Guitar Solo: Ride Cymbal Walking-Feel, using 2-Bar Timekeeping Clichés
4. **One Chorus** of the Head: Two-Feel on the Sock Cymbals (comping the head);
   Tagging the Turnaround 3x to end

Unit Five: Rhythm Changes Form

Scan for bio.

Jeff "Tain" Watts

Description

In this unit, you will learn to play an AABA 32-bar form with both a two-feel and walking-feel. Trading fours (with select four-bar solo concentrations) will also be presented.

Upon completion of this unit, you should be able to:

- Play a two-feel in the A section(s) and a walking-feel in the B section of an AABA form
- Be able to trade fours while using select four-bar solo concentrations

Chapter 1: 32-Bar AABA Rhythm Changes Form

"Rhythm Changes" is a 32-bar AABA form that is based on the chord changes of George Gershwin's popular jazz standard "I Got Rhythm." These chord changes have been used numerous times (throughout the 1930s, '40s, and '50s) to form new (usually uptempo) jazz compositions. In addition, this "Rhythm Changes" slang refers to the first four chords (I, VI, ii, V) of the jazz progression in Letter A and shifting dominant 7th chords (III7, VI7, II7, V7) in Letter B.

Example 5.1

This AABA form is comprised of two sections, and each one is assigned a rehearsal letter (A or B). Both letters (sections) represent three key musical attributes:

- An eight-bar phrase
- A unique melody and chord structure
- A different rhythm (or groove)

Let's examine each key element individually:

1. An eight-bar phrase

Each letter denotes the use of an eight-bar phrase (or section).

Example 5.2

2. A unique melody and chord progression

Both letters are also centered on a melody and chord progression. In this case, the A section utilizes a unique (and dense) melody and a I, VI, ii, V chord progression. The B section clearly differs by using ensemble figures through a III7, VI7, II7, V7 chord progression.

Example 5.3
Melody 1, Letter A:

Melody 2, Letter B:

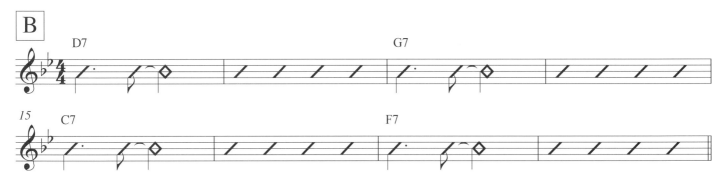

3. A different rhythm (groove)

As stated earlier, there are two letters (and melodies) within this form. Each one needs its own particular rhythm (or groove). As a result, there are two different grooves present within this chart.
The A section features a two-feel on the sock cymbal (hi-hat).

Example 5.4

The B section groove features a walking-feel on the ride cymbal, with the bass drum feathering quarter notes, and the hi-hat foot closing on beats 2 and 4.

Example 5.5

Therefore, the entire head would be played like this:

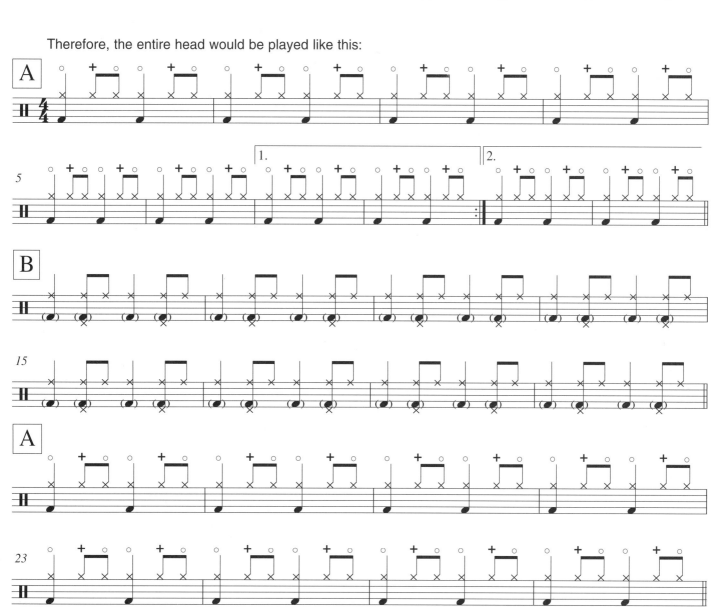

Chorus of Instrumental Solo: Marking the Form with the Walking-Feel

During the solo sections of an AABA Rhythm Changes tune, it is customary to "walk" through the entire form on the ride cymbal. Although, you still need to mark the song's form by outlining (and drawing attention to) each *different* section. This "marking" is accomplished by changing ride cymbals for each section. (In jazz, all cymbals are considered rides.) Therefore, the A section should have a particular cymbal/ texture and the B section should also have a different cymbal/texture.

During the "walking" instrumental solo, the following form, performance instructions, and cymbal will be used:

1. Letter A (2x)—Ride Cymbal 1

2. Letter B (Ride Cymbal 2)

3. Letter A (1x)—(Ride Cymbal 1)

Ending the Song: Tagging the Last Two Bars

During the last A (within the Head), it is customary to tag the last two bars of the song three times to form a definitive ending:

Chapter 2: Trading Fours in an AABA – Four-Bar Concentration

Just as in a 12-bar blues, the Rhythm Changes form also has a strong tradition in improvisation and rudimental manipulation. Therefore, this chapter's lesson features (five) four-bar solo concentrations in the style of Philly Joe Jones. Once mastered, these concepts will be utilized within this unit's 32-bar tune while trading one chorus of "fours."

Four-Bar No. 1—The "2" above each eighth-note grouping denotes that they are to be played as straight eighth notes.

Track 34
(Ex. 5.6-5.10) Example 5.6

Four-Bar No. 2

Example 5.7

Four-Bar No. 3—The "2" above each eighth-note grouping denotes that they are to be played as straight eighth notes. Notice the paradiddle-diddle in measure 2 and the 5-stroke roll in measure 3:

Example 5.8

Four-Bar No. 4

Example 5.9

Four-Bar No. 5

Example 5.10

Trading Fours

Again, trading fours is a time-honored tradition of soloing between jazz instrumentalists and drummers. "Fours" are mini four-bar solos, which are traded (alternated) between an instrumentalist (or group of instrumentalists) and the drummer. These occur within a song's form. In the following example, the drums trade fours through one chorus of a 32-bar (Rhythm Changes) form. Four eight-bar phrases can be traded within each chorus. Therefore, the instrumentalist (in this case guitar) begins each section and the drums finish it. For example:

Example 5.11

If you were to play Four-Bar No. 5 in the first Letter A, Four-Bar No. 4 in Letter B, and Four-Bar No.2 in the last A, it would be played like this:

Track 35

Example 5.12

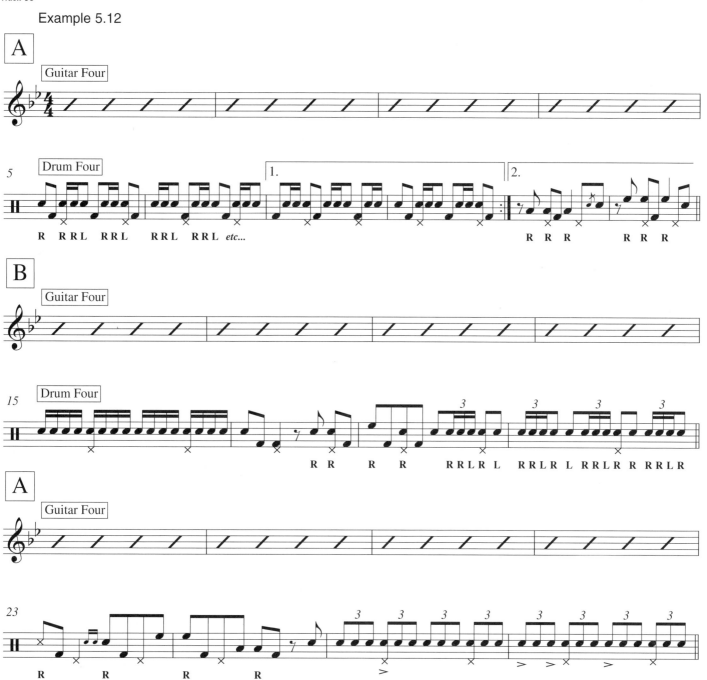

For the sake of brevity, I have omitted another four-bar concentration within the second letter A (within the chorus above). However, in a real performance setting, an alternate solo idea should be used.

During the last A (within the Head), it is customary to tag the last two bars of an AABA three additional times (four times total) to form a definitive ending.

Chapter 3: The Chart and Play-Along

Track 36 Demo
Track 37 Play-Along

Example 5.13

Form:
1. **Head:** The two-feel sock for **Letter A** and ride cymbal walking-feel for **Letter B**
2. **Chorus** of Guitar Solo (all walking-feel on the ride cymbal; Letter A ride cymbal 1 and Letter B ride cymbal 2)
3. **Chorus** of Trading Fours
4. **Head:** The two-feel sock for **Letter A** and ride cymbal walking-feel for **Letter B**
5. **Outro/Ending:** Tagging the last two bars 3x (Ride Cymbal 1)

Unit Six: ABAB Form

Scan for bio.

Joe Morello

Description

In this unit, you will learn to comp the melody within an ABAB 32-bar form with both long and short notes. Rudimental applications of the single drag will also be presented.

Upon completion of this unit, you should be able to:
- Accentuate and comp with long and short notes
- Understand and use the eighth-note rule for consecutive eighth notes
- Be able to play select voicings of the single drag on the kit

Chapter 1: 32-Bar ABAB Form

The ABAB 32-bar form is based on a theme (A) and variation (B). This song form is notated as a 16-bar form that repeats, for a total of 32 bars. For example:

Example 6.1

Just as in Unit 5, this ABAB form is comprised of two different sections, and each one is assigned a rehearsal letter (A or B). Each letter (section) represents three key musical attributes:

- An eight-bar phrase
- A unique melody and chord structure
- A different rhythm, ride surface, or groove

So how does this information apply to the Unit 6 tune? Well, let's examine each key element individually:

1. An eight-bar phrase
Each letter denotes the use of an eight-bar phrase (or section).

Example 6.2

2. A unique melody and chord progression

Each letter is also centered on a melody and chord progression. In this case, the A section utilizes a unique (and dense) melody and a I, VI, ii, V chord progression. The B section clearly differs by using ensemble figures through a III7, VI7, II7, V7 chord progression.

Example 6.3

Melody 1 – Letter A:

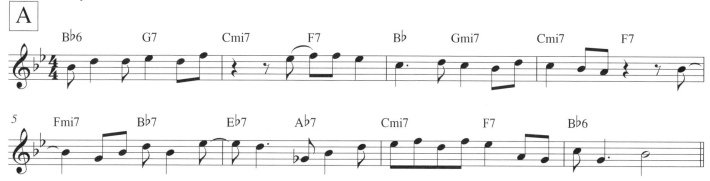

Melody 2 – Letter B:

3. A different rhythm (groove)

As stated earlier, there are two letters (and melodies) within this form. Each one needs its own particular rhythm, ride surface, or groove. This chart has a walking-feel through the entire chart, so you will need to switch ride cymbals for each section.

The **A section** features a walking-feel on the first ride cymbal.

Example 6.4

The **B section** groove features a walking-feel on the second ride cymbal.

Example 6.5

Chorus of the Head and Guitar Solo—Marking the Form with the Walking-Feel

During each section of an ABAB, it is customary to "walk" through the entire form on the ride cymbal. Although (and just like Unit 5), you still need to mark the song's form by outlining (and drawing attention to) each *different* section. This "marking" is accomplished by employing sonic changes to the drumset, and also by changing ride cymbals for each section.For example:

Example 6.6

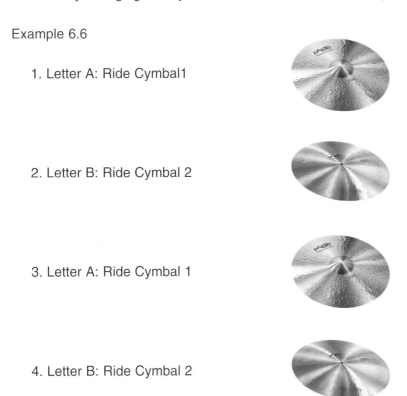

1. Letter A: Ride Cymbal1

2. Letter B: Ride Cymbal 2

3. Letter A: Ride Cymbal 1

4. Letter B: Ride Cymbal 2

Ending the Song: Tagging the Last Two Bars

During the last B (within the head), it is customary to tag the last two bars of the song three times to form a definitive ending:

Example 6.7

Chapter 2: Comping the Head – Long and Short Notes

During the head, the drums support the melody line by accompanying and accentuating notes within each phrase. These are articulated by note duration, and they can be accented by either the snare drum or bass drum. The ride cymbal pattern and hi-hat should remain unchanged. In this unit, you should voice the head's short (eighth) notes on the snare drum and long notes (tied eighth, quarter, and dotted-quarter notes) on the bass drum. For example:

Example 6.8

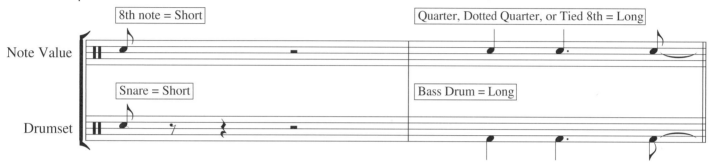

Therefore, if you were to play the entire A section (while following this method), it would be played like this:

Comping Each Note within the A Section's Melody

Track 38

Example 6.9

Playing each note within the melody, however, is impractical and unmusical. Therefore, we will employ the Eighth-Note Rule that states the following:

Eighth-Note Rule

When you are reading consecutive eighth notes, you should not play every eighth note; rather, play the first, the last, or first *and* last of each grouping. Therefore, if you were to play the entire A section (while following the Eighth-Note Rule and proper drumset voicings from example 6.9), it would be played like this:

Comping the Eighth-Note Rule within the A Section's Melody

Track 39

Example 6.10

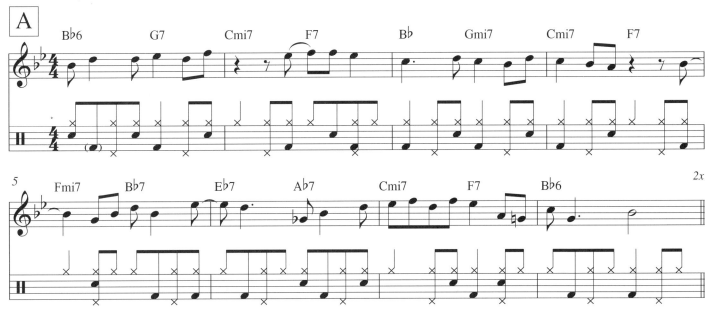

Comping the B Section

Now that you understand both the proper drumset voicings and the Eighth-Note Rule, write your own proper comping ideas for the B section's head below:

Example 6.11

Chapter 3: The Single Drag

The ruff is a combination of grace notes and a stroke. **It is played with the same motion as the flam (Unit 2)**. The stroke is made with an arm and wrist movement, while the grace notes are made alone with the wrist (or fingers). The ruff is written by placing two small grace notes before the large note. The purpose of the ruff is to broaden the sound and tone of a drum.

Example 6.12

The ruff is named from the hand that plays the principal note. There are three types of ruffs: the right ruff, left ruff, and alternating ruffs. Alternating ruffs are played from hand to hand, and the hand that plays the last stroke (of the first ruff) stays close to the drum to be in position to play the grace note of the second (following) ruff.

Example 6.13

Alternating Ruffs

Start with the right stick high and the bead of the left stick two inches above the drumhead. Play the grace note with an upstroke and play the main stroke with a downstroke. Your sticks are now prepared (and in position) to play the next ruff. When playing ruffs, one hand should always be raised higher than the other hand.

Example 6.14

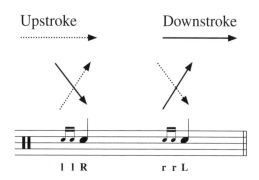

For additional motion information, refer to Unit 2 (examples 2.4–2.7). Ruffs and Flams both follow the same movements.

Ruff Rudiment: The Single Drag

The Single Drag is comprised of two grace notes and two principal notes. This hand-to-hand rudiment is usually played as a three-note grouping in 3/4 time. Many drummers also use the Single Drag to replace a 5-stroke roll in extremely fast playing situations.

Example 6.15

Just as in the Alternating Flams and Ruffs, this rudiment's motion also utilizes upstrokes and downstrokes to prepare for the next hand's stroke.

Example 6.16

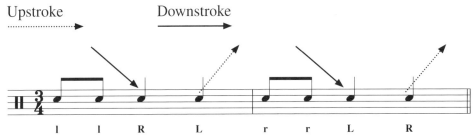

Phrasing in 4/4

In order to use this rudiment within a 4/4 jazz context, we must take this three-note grouping and phrase it as swung eighth notes, which are a two-note grouping. The hi-hat is played on beats 2 and 4:

Example 6.17

Track 40

By using the Single Drag in this manner, the rudiment becomes a three-measure phrase, which is also the basis for a 3-against-4 accent structure. (You will notice that the fourth bar is identical to the first.) The hi-hat foot also aids in developing this jazz 4/4 pulse as well.

Chapter 4: Trading Fours

Phrasing in 4/4: Additional Jazz Drum Voicing

Obviously, there are hundreds of ways to voice this three-note rudiment on the drumkit. I have listed some of the most traditional options below:

1. Single Drag on the Toms:

In this example, the drags are played on the snare, and the remaining notes are played on the high tom (left hand) and floor tom (right hand). The hi-hat is played on beats 2 and 4.

Track 41
(Ex. 6.18-6.19)

Example 6.18

2. Single Drag on Bass Drum and Cymbals:

In this example, the left-hand notes are played on the crash, and the right-hand notes are played on ride cymbal (both cymbals are reinforced with the bass drum). The drag notes remain on the snare, and the hi-hat is played on beats 2 and 4.

Example 6.19

In the following example, the drums trade fours through one chorus of a 32-bar ABAB form. There are two four-bar phrases that can be traded within each rehearsal letter.

Example 6.20

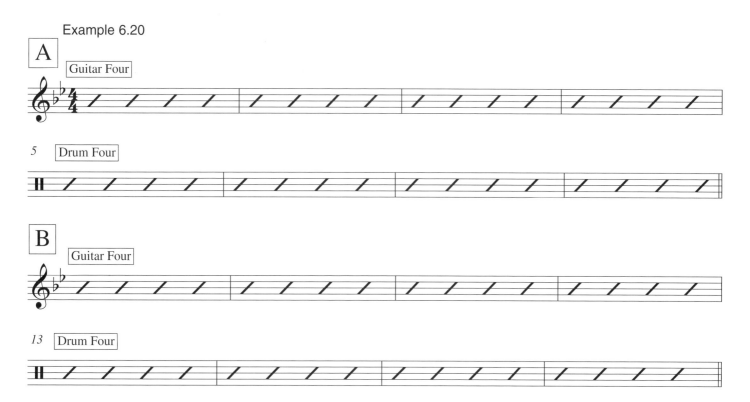

Trading Fours with the Single Drag Voicings

If you were to use the last chapter's Single Drag phrases (ex. 6.17–6.19) while trading one chorus of "fours" in an ABAB, it would be played like this:

Track 42

Example 6.21

Chapter 5: The Chart and Play-Along

Track 43 Demo
Track 44 Play-Along

Example 6.22

Form:

1. **Head**

    a. **Letter A** (Ride Cymbal 1): Comping the head (melody)

    b. **Letter B** (Ride Cymbal 2): Comping the head (melody)

2. **Chorus** of Guitar Solo—Switching Rides for Each A and B

3. **Chorus** of Trading Fours: Using the Single Drag Voicings

4. **Head**

    a. **Letter A** (Ride Cymbal 1): Comping the head (melody)

    b. **Letter B** (Ride Cymbal 2): Comping the head (melody)

5. **Outro/Ending:** Tag the last two bars of letter B 3 additional times (4x total; Ride Cymbal 2) to form a definitive ending.

Unit Seven: Triplets and Bass Vamps

Scan for bio.

Ed Thigpen

Description

In this unit, you will learn to comp the melody as triplets over a minor blues and a vamp bass line. Timekeeping clichés within this feel will also be presented.

Upon completion of this unit, you should be able to:

- Comp in triplets
- Understand a vamp
- Understand and use triplet timekeeping clichés
- Be able to play select voicings of the bass line and melody within triplet comping

Chapter 1: Vamp Bass Line Basics

This unit's tune is a 12-bar minor blues, and it features a bass line vamp. This type of bass pattern is very repetitive, but it does not follow a typical two-feel or walking pattern. It is a two-bar phrase and played at a medium to slow tempo.

Example 7.1

Triplet Comping

Performing this bass line at a slow tempo allows the band (and soloist) the opportunity to improvise freely through (and over) this rhythmic motif. Due to this tempo, many drummers forgo comping with eighth notes and phrase in eighth-note triplets instead.

Example 7.2

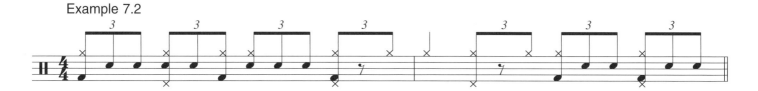

Grand Staff Lead Sheet

As there is both a notated melody and bass line for this tune, a grand staff is used. The melody (Head) is placed on the top staff (treble clef) and the bass line is present on the bottom staff (bass clef).

Example 7.3

Chapter 2: Triplet Comping

Preliminary Exercises

In order for you to become fluent in playing triplet comping figures, I have listed several preliminary exercises. Work through them from 60–70 bpm, with an eighth-note triplet click.

Track 45

Example 7.4

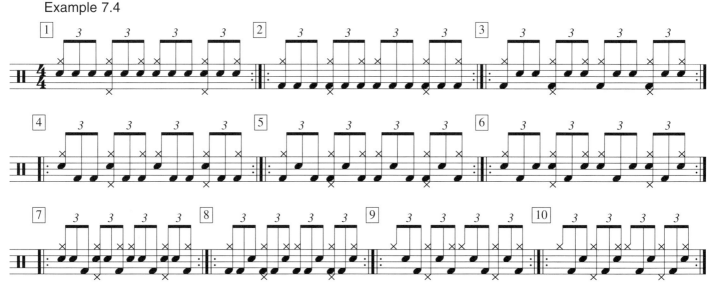

Applying Comping to the Vamp

Now, let's use our newfound triplet independence to play some comping figures through the vamp bass line and the head. The drums will comp alongside the bass for the first eight measures, and in bars 9 and 10, they will follow the melody. Finally, in bars 11 and 12, the drums return to the original bass motif.

If you comped in traditional swung eighths, it would be played as follows:

Eighth-Note Comping

Track 46

Example 7.5

However (and at slow tempos), it is much more appropriate to comp in eighth-note triplets. With this in mind, we are going to develop two methods for comping within the vamp bass line and head.

1. Triplet Comping: Bass Drum Lead

In the following example, you will play each rhythm with the bass drum while filling in eighth-note triplets on the snare. The ride cymbal rhythm should remain constant with the hi-hat foot closing on 2 and 4. Notice how the drum comping transitions from the bass line (in bars 1–8) to the Head figures (on bars 9 and 10).

Track 47
(Ex. 7.6-7.7) Example 7.6

2. Triplet Comping: Snare Drum Lead

In the following example, you will play each rhythm with the snare drum while filling in eighth-note triplets on the bass drum. The ride cymbal rhythm should remain constant with the hi-hat foot closing on 2 and 4. Again, notice how the drum comping switches from the bass line (in bars 1–8) to the Head figures (on bars 9 and 10).

Example 7.7

Chapter 3: Comping Clichés

Comping Behind a Soloist (Choruses of Solo)

Just as with eighth-note comping, our most important job is to mark phrases and sections. With this in mind, I have listed the shouldered ride articulation and triplet comping clichés for you below:

Example 7.8

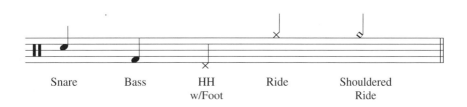

Timekeeping Clichés

Let's use our newfound triplet independence to play some musical comping clichés:

Track 48
(Ex. 7.9-7.10) Example 7.9

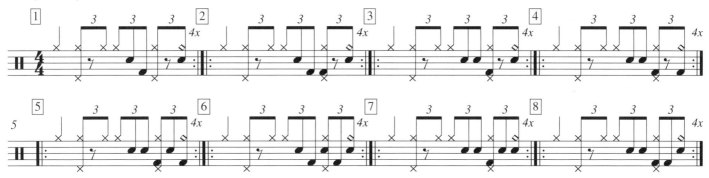

Clichés within a Form

Once numbers 1–8 are comfortable, put them into a four-bar phrase like this:

Example 7.10

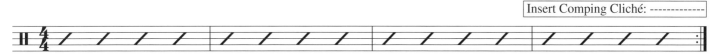

If you picked number 1 and used it within this form, it would be played like this:

Example 7.11

Chapter 4: The Chart and Play-Along

Track 49 Demo
Track 50 Play-Along

Example 7.12

Form:

1. **2 Choruses** of the Head (over the vamp bass line)
2. **2 Choruses** of Guitar Solo: Switching to another ride
3. **1 Chorus** of the Head
4. **Outro/Ending:** Tag the turnaround (bars 9–12) 3 additional times (4 times total) to form a definitive ending.

Unit Eight: 6/8 Afro-Cuban Feel

8

Bill Stewart

Scan for bio.

Description

In this unit, you will learn about 6/8 Afro Cuban and how to use it within a triplet jazz feel. Timekeeping clichés part 2 and using the hi-hat as a melodic voice will also be presented.

Upon completion of this unit, you should be able to:
- Understand the 6/8 folkloric feel
- Play a 6/8 Afro Cuban-inspired groove as triplets
- Understand and use triplet timekeeping clichés part 2
- Use the hi-hat as a melodic comping voice

Chapter 1: Origins of the 6/8 Feel

Many of the fundamental rhythms used in West Africa and Cuba are based on 6/8 feels. In Cuba, one popular 6/8 feel is known as **bembe**. This folkloric feel (and rhythm) gets its name from the word *bembes*, which are religious gatherings that include drumming, singing, and dancing. In order to understand this feel, let's take a look at each instrument within the traditional folkloric feel.

Afro-Cuban 6/8 Folkloric Feel

During a religious gathering, the bembe (folkloric feel) is played on a hoe blade, high drum, low drum, and a shekere (a hollowed out gourd with beads wrapped around it). This feel, played in Cuba, is completely African in style and instrumentation. Let's take a look at each part in detail:

Example 8.1

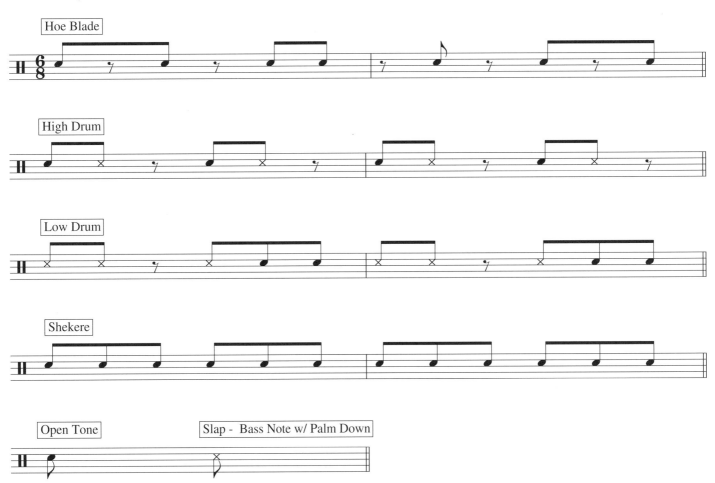

Note: Similar rhythms are used throughout West Africa, especially in Nigeria, where most of Cuba's African population originated.

6/8 Clave Pattern: The Key

Clave is a Spanish word meaning "key." The clave is the key to the rhythmic feel being played, and it is the skeletal rhythmic figure around which other drums and percussion instruments are played. Here is the 6/8 clave:

Example 8.2

In order to feel this pattern, try playing your hi-hat foot on dotted quarter notes:

Example 8.3

6/8 Bell Pattern

The 6/8 clave is the foundation for the 6/8-bell pattern. Notice that this pattern is actually the clave figure with one additional note in each bar:

Example 8.4

6/8 Afro-Cuban Full Drumset

The full drumset groove utilizes the folkloric high tom, low tom, and the 6/8 bell (hoe blade) rhythms. Each rhythm is voiced like this:

Example 8.5

Folkloric		Drumset
High Drum	=	Bass Drum
Low Drum	=	Rack Tom
Hoe Blade (6/8 Bell)	=	Ride Cymbal

Altogether, it is played like this:

Example 8.6

Notice the cross-stick note in each bar.

Chapter 2: Using the Naningo within 4/4

In jazz, many drummers such as Elvin Jones, Tony Williams, and Roy Haynes used this 6/8 pattern within a 4/4 context. This was accomplished by translating the two-bar 6/8 groove into a one-bar pattern as triplets in 4/4. Oftentimes this is referred to as a 6/8 Afro Cuban feel.

Two-Bar 6/8 Pattern

Example 8.7

Track 51
(Ex. 8.7-8.8)

One-Bar 4/4 Pattern as Triplets: *The 6/8 Afro Cuban Feel*

Although written in 4/4, many musicians refer to this groove as a 6/8 Afro Cuban feel.

Example 8.8

Preliminary Exercises

In order to become fluent in playing this pattern, I have listed several preliminary exercises for you to practice. You will also notice that the hi-hat is closing on beats 2 and 4, which solidifies the jazz timekeeping feel. With an eighth-note triplet click, work through these examples from 60–70 bpm.

Example 8.9

Applying the 6/8 Afro Cuban Feel to the Head

Now, let's use our newfound triplet pattern to groove through the head of Unit 8's tune. The bass will play a walking (quarter note) feel through this head. You should play the head like this:

Example 8.10

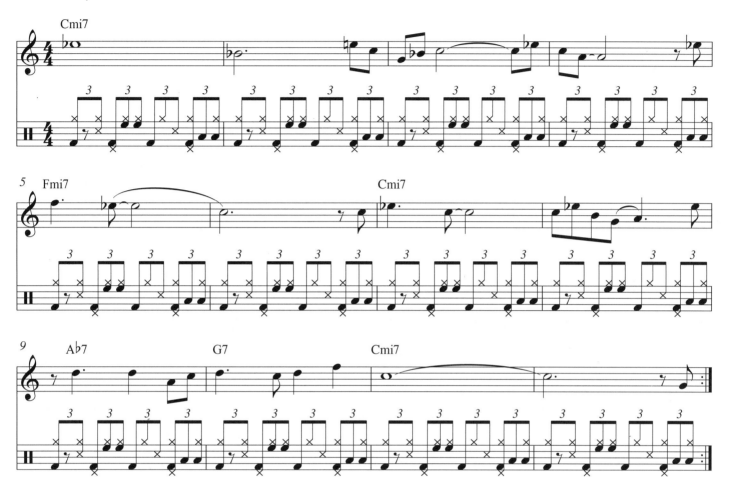

Chapter 3: Triplet Comping and Clichés Part 2

Return to the Vamp

In the choruses of guitar (or instrumental) solo, this unit's tune will return to the original vamp bass line. With this in mind, I have listed some additional preliminary exercises to help you further your triplet comping vocabulary. These now include using the middle triplet and left-hand snare buzzes on select beats.

Notation addition: Snare buzz

 Example 8.11

Track 52

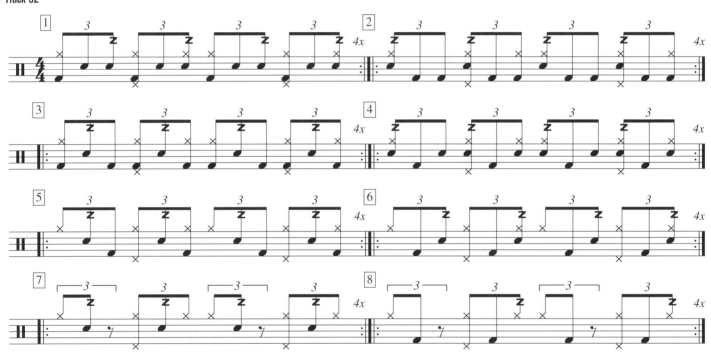

Comping Clichés 2: Behind a Soloist (Choruses of Solo)

To review, our most important job is to mark phrases and sections. With this in mind, I have listed some new triplet comping clichés (and shouldered ride articulations) for you below:

Track 53
(Ex. 8.12-8.13)

Example 8.12

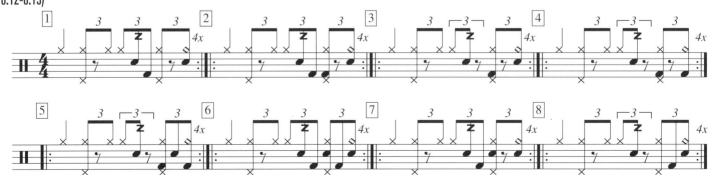

Unit Eight: 6/8 Afro-Cuban Feel

Clichés within a Form

Once numbers 1–8 are comfortable, use them within a four-bar phrase.

Example 8.13

Therefore, exercise 1 would be played like this:

Musical Ideas Based on the Vamp

I have listed some additional musical ideas (based on the vamp figure) to help you further your triplet comping vocabulary. Try to use these within the choruses of solo and vamp feel.

Example 8.14

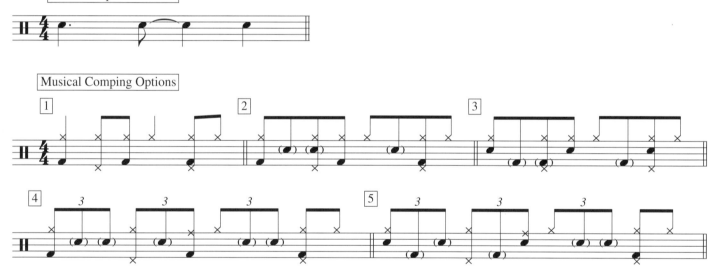

Using the Hi-Hat as a Comping Voice

Many drummers also use the hi-hat as a melodic (comping) voice within triplet comping and vamp bass lines. With this in mind, I have listed some examples for you:

 Example 8.15

Track 54

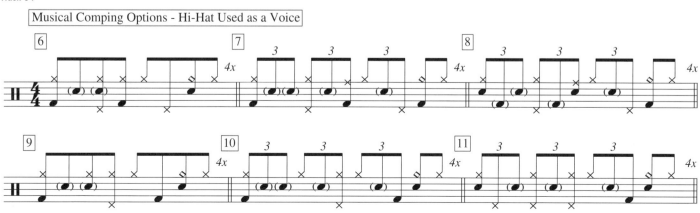

83

Chapter 4: The Chart and Play-Along

Track 55 Demo
Track 56 Play-Along

Example 8.16

Form:

1. **2 Choruses** of the Head (over the Naningo and walking bass line)
2. **2 Choruses** of Guitar Solo: (over the original bass line vamp). Switching to another ride
3. **1 Chorus** of the Head: (over the Naningo and walking bass line)
4. **Outro/Ending:** Tag the turnaround (bars 9–12) 2 additional times (3 times total) to form a definitive ending.

Unit Nine: Jazz Waltz

Scan for bio.

Elvin Jones

Description

In this unit, you will learn about the 3/4 jazz waltz and how to use it within a "one" and "three" feel. Additional timekeeping clichés in 3/4 will also be presented.

Upon completion of this unit, you should be able to:

- Understand the 3/4 jazz waltz feel
- Play a 3/4 waltz in both a "one" and a "three" feel
- Understand and use waltz timekeeping clichés
- Use the hi-hat as a melodic comping voice

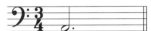

Chapter 1: 3/4 Waltz Timekeeping

Many jazz standards are written and performed within the 3/4 time signature. This time feel is called a waltz, and there are two common rhythmic approaches employed. They are:

1. In "one"
In this feel, the bass player plays a dotted half note on beat 1.

Example 9.1

2. In "three"
In this feel, the bassist plays a quarter-note pulse that forms a walking pattern. (This is very similar to a 4/4 walking feel.)

Example 9.2

Drumset Voices within a 3/4 Feel

Just as in 4/4 jazz timekeeping, there are three main components that make up the 3/4 waltz: bass drum, ride cymbal, and hi-hat. Let's take a look at each in detail:

1. The Bass Drum
The bass drum follows the bassist's feel (as discussed in the examples above), and feathers within the following patterns:

Example 9.3

In "one"   **In "three"**

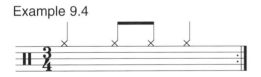

2. The Ride Cymbal Pattern
Usually, you will play this ride cymbal pattern:

Example 9.4

3. The Hi-Hat
The hi-hat can utilize any of the following four rhythms:

Example 9.5

Preliminary Exercises

In order for you to become fluent in playing the waltz pattern, I have listed several preliminary exercises. Work through these examples from 60–70 bpm alongside an eighth-note triplet click.

The Hi-Hat and Ride Alone

Track 57
(Ex. 9.6-9.8)
Example 9.6

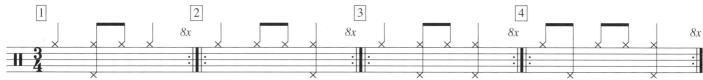

In "one"
Example 9.7

In "three"
Example 9.8

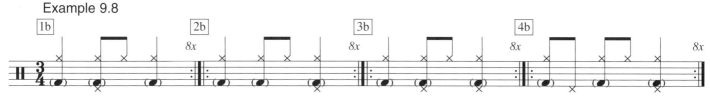

Clichés within a Form

Once the preliminary exercises (9.7 and 9.8) are comfortable, put each into a four-bar phrase like this:

Track 58 Example 9.9

If you picked exercise 1b (from example 9.8) and used it within this form, it would be played like this:
Example 9.10

Alongside a Bass Line

In order to master these ideas, please practice the cliché forms from examples 9.9 and 9.10 alongside a waltz bass line practice track:

Example 9.11

Track 59

Note: This is an example of a walking bass line. (The track elaborates on this theme.)

Chapter 2: Applying 3/4 Feels to the Chart

Now, let's apply our waltz timekeeping to the head of this 32-bar ABAB tune. The A section has a "one" feel and the B section has a "three" feel.

Example 9.12

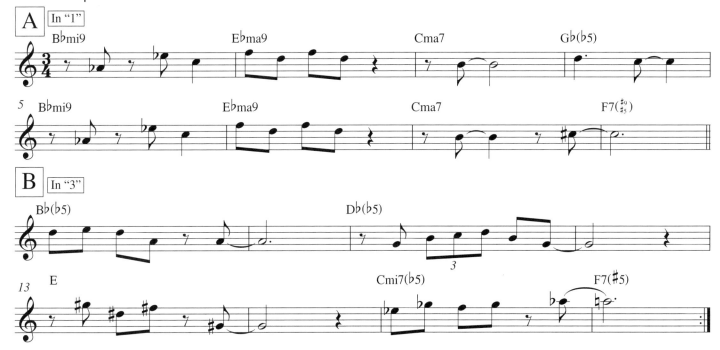

During the A section, your bass drum will feather on beat 1 of each measure like this:

Example 9.13

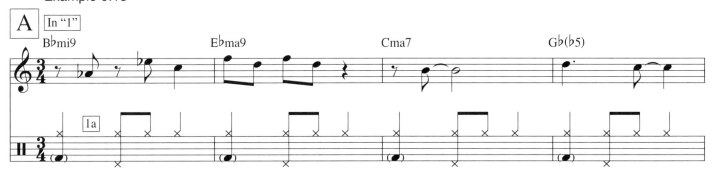

Any hi-hat pattern from the previous pages is acceptable.

During the B section, your bass drum will feather quarter notes like this:

Example 9.14

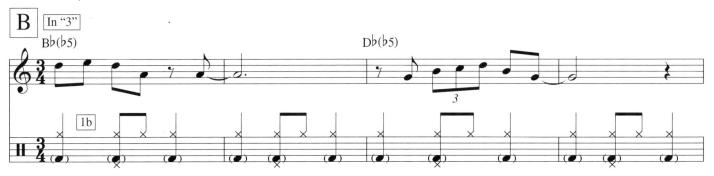

Any hi-hat pattern from the previous pages is acceptable.

In addition, you will switch ride surfaces for each section (letter) like this:

Example 9.15

Letter A (Ride Cymbal 1)

Letter B (Ride Cymbal 2)

Choruses of Solo: Timekeeping Clichés in a "Three" Feel

The choruses of guitar (or instrumental) solo utilize a "three" feel for both sections. Therefore, I have listed many additional preliminary exercises to help further your 3/4 comping vocabulary.

Example 9.16

Track 60

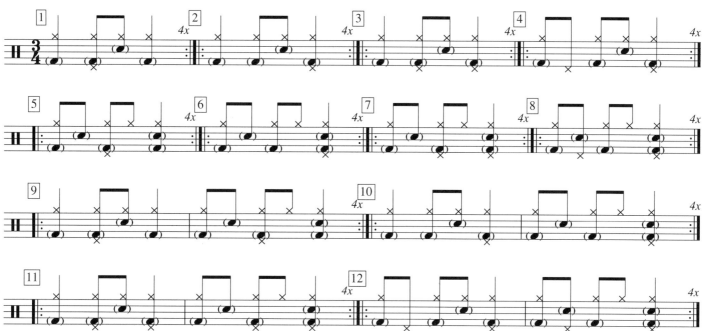

The Ending

You will end this chart by playing the last two bars of Letter B three times. This will form a definitive ending.

Example 9.17

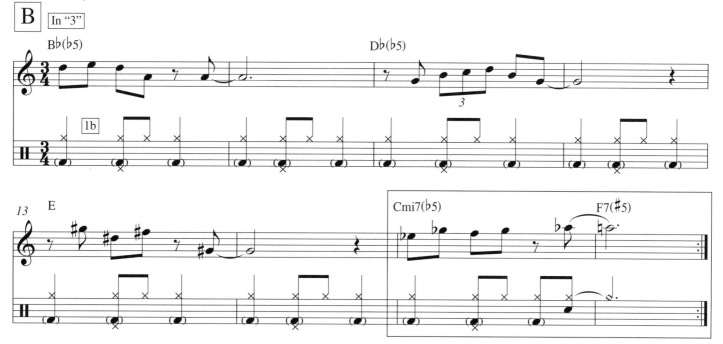

Chapter 3: The Chart and Play-Along

Track 61 Demo
Track 62 Play-Along

Example 9.18

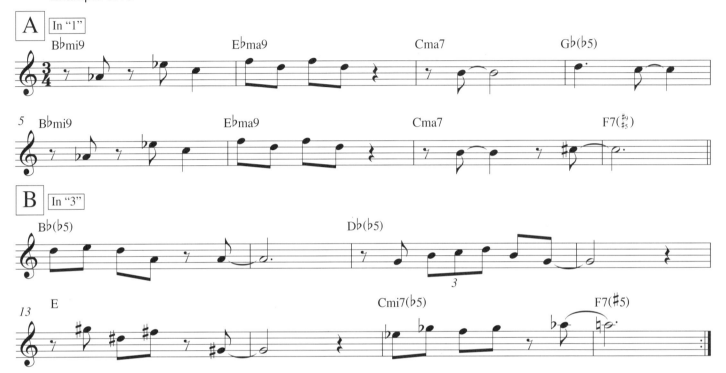

Form:

1. **Head:** Letter A in "one" and letter B in "three"
2. **(2) Choruses** of Guitar Solo in "three," switching ride surfaces for each section. See example 9.15
3. **Head:** Letter A in "one" and letter B in "three"
4. **Outro/Ending:** Tag the last two bars of letter B 3 additional times (4 times total) to form a definitive ending.

Unit Ten: Broken Three Feel

Scan for bio.

Brian Blade

Description

In this unit, you will learn to use the 3/4 waltz "broken three" feel within an ABAB tune. Trading fours and comping the Head will also be presented.

Upon completion of this unit, you should be able to:
- Trade fours within the 3/4 time signature and ABAB tune
- Comp the head in 3/4

Chapter 1: 3/4 Waltz Timekeeping II

As we discussed in Unit 9, many popular jazz standards are written (and performed) within the 3/4 time signature. In this unit, we will expand our 3/4 studies and utilize a waltz "broken three" feel.

The "Broken Three" Feel
In this feel, the bassist plays a dotted-quarter note pulse.

Example 10.1

Drumset Voices within the 3/4 Broken Feel
Just as with the "one" and "three" feels, there are three main components that make up a "broken three" feel. They are:

1. The Bass Drum
The bass drum follows the bassist's feel (as shown in the example above) and feathers a dotted-quarter pulse:

Example 10.2

2. The Ride Cymbal
Usually, you will play this ride cymbal pattern within a "broken three" feel:

Example 10.3

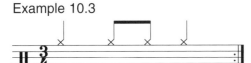

3. The Hi-Hat
The hi-hat can utilize any of these four rhythms:

Example 10.4

Track 63

4. All Together
Example 10.5

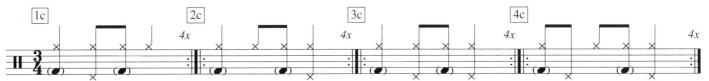

92

In order for you to become fluent in playing the "broken three" waltz pattern, I have listed several preliminary exercises. Work through these examples from 60–70 bpm alongside an eighth-note triplet click.

Track 64

Example 10.6

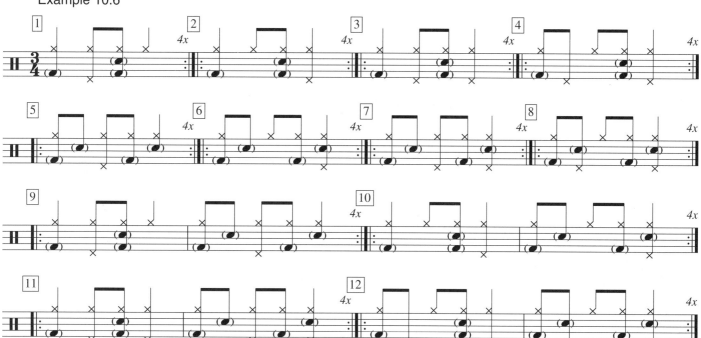

Clichés within the Form

Once the preliminary exercises (example 10.6) are comfortable, put each into a four-bar phrase like this:

Example 10.7

Insert Preliminary Exercise Here:

Therefore, if you used exercise 1 (from example 10.6) within this form, it would be played like this:

Example 10.8

Alongside a Bass Line

In order to master these ideas, practice the cliché forms from example 10.6 alongside a waltz bass line practice track.

Track 65

Example 10.9

Note: This is an example of a broken feel bass line. (The track elaborates on this theme.)

Chapter 2: Applying 3/4 Feels to the Chart

Now, let's apply our "broken three" waltz timekeeping to the head of this 32-bar ABAB tune. Both sections utilize this dotted-quarter feel:

Example 10.10

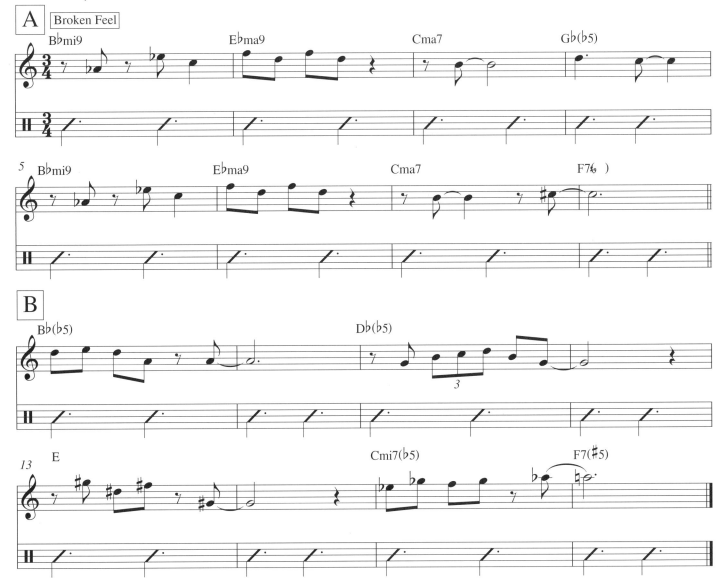

During both sections, your bass drum will feather on beats 1 and the "&" of beat 2. If you used exercise 1 from Example 10.6, the head would be played like this:

Example 10.11

Any hi-hat pattern from the previous pages is acceptable.

Example 10.12

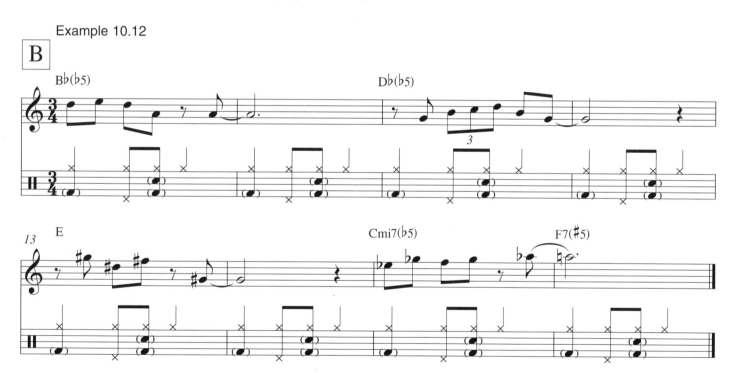

Any hi-hat pattern from the previous pages is acceptable.

Choruses of Solo: Timekeeping Clichés in a "Three" Feel

Just as in Unit 9's chart, the choruses of guitar (or instrumental) solo utilize a walking "three" feel for both sections. Therefore, I have listed many triplet-based preliminary exercises to help further your 3/4 comping vocabulary.

Track 66

Example 10.13

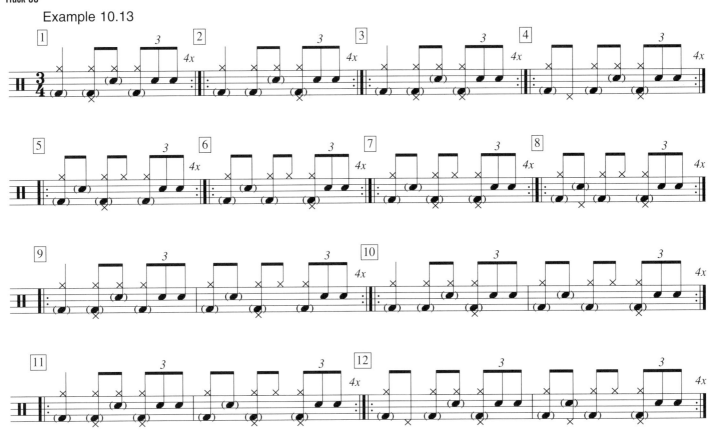

Chapter 3: Flam Accent No. 1, Single Drag, and Paradiddle in 3/4

This chapter features four 3/4 interpretations of the Flam Accent, Single Drag, and Single Paradiddle. Once mastered, you will trade two choruses of "fours" within this unit's ABAB tune.

Flam Rudiment: Flam Accent No.1—Traditional 6/8

The Flam Accent No. 1 is usually played as a three-note grouping in 6/8 time.

Example 10.14

Flam Accent No. 1—Swung Eighth Notes in 3/4

In order to use this rudiment within a 3/4 jazz context, we must phrase this three-note grouping as a two-note grouping, i.e., swung eighth notes. The hi-hat should be played on beat 2.

Track 67
(Ex. 10.15-10.18)

Example 10.15

Phrasing in 3/4: Additional Jazz Drum Voicing

Obviously, there are hundreds of ways to voice this three-note rudiment on the drumkit. I have listed some of the most traditional options below:

1. Flams on the Toms:

In this example, the Left Flam is played on the high tom and the Right Flam is played on the floor tom. The unaccented notes remain on the snare, and the hi-hat is played on beat 2.

Example 10.16

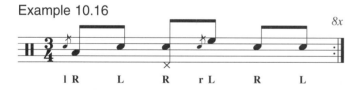

2. Flams on Bass Drum and Cymbals:

In this example, the Left Flam is played on the crash cymbal, and the Right Flam is played on ride cymbal **(both cymbals are reinforced with the bass drum)**. The unaccented notes remain on the snare, and the hi-hat is played on beat 2.

Example 10.17

3. Timekeeping Flam Accent:

In this example, you will play the coordination pattern from example 10.6 (exercise 1). However, in this timekeeping variation, the left hand remains on the snare, and the right hand plays on the ride cymbal. You will play the Flam Accent (in a traditional timekeeping position) while reinforcing both Flams with the bass drum. The hi-hat is played on beat 2.

Example 10.18

Ruff Rudiment: The Single Drag

The Single Drag is comprised of two grace notes and two principal notes. It is usually played as a three-note grouping in 3/4 time. It is also a hand-to-hand rudiment. In extremely fast playing situations, many drummers use the Single Drag to replace a 5-stroke roll.

Track 68
(Ex. 10.19-10.22)

Example 10.19

Phrasing in 3/4: Additional Jazz Drum Voicing

In order to use this rudiment within a 3/4 jazz context, we must phrase this four-note grouping as a syncopated grouping, i.e., as swung eighth notes. The hi-hat is played on beat 2.

Example 10.20

Additional Jazz Drum Voicing

Obviously, there are hundreds of ways to voice this three-note rudiment on the drumkit. I have listed some of the most traditional options:

1. Single Drag on the Toms:

In this example, the ruffs are played on the snare, and the remaining notes are played on the high tom (left hand) and floor tom (right hand). The hi-hat is played on beat 2.

Example 10.21

2. Single Drag on Bass Drum and Cymbals:

In this example, the left-hand notes are played on the crash, and the right-hand notes are played on ride cymbal **(both cymbals are reinforced with the bass drum)**. The drag notes remain on the snare, and the hi-hat is played on beat 2.

Example 10.22

l l R   L   r r L   R

New Rudiment: The Abbreviated Single Paradiddle

The Single Paradiddle is comprised of four main notes and two principal notes. Normally, the Single Paradiddle is a "hand-to-hand" rudiment in 4/4, which leads with the right hand and then follows with the left hand. Many jazz drummers have modified the Single Paradiddle to lead exclusively with the right hand, which makes it very useable within 3/4 time.

Track 69
(Ex. 10.23-10.26)

Example 10.23

R   L   R   R   L

Phrasing in 3/4: Additional Jazz Drum Voicing

Obviously, there are hundreds of ways to voice the Abbreviated Single Paradiddle on the drumkit. I have listed some of the most traditional options below:

1. Single Paradiddle on the Toms:

In this example, the Abbreviated Single Paradiddle is played on the snare and the remaining notes are played on the high tom (left hand) and floor tom (right hand). The hi-hat is played on beat 2.

Example 10.24

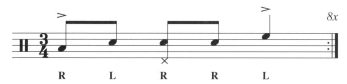

R   L   R   R   L

2. The Abbreviated Single Paradiddle—Bass Drum and Cymbals:

In this example, the left-hand notes are played on the crash and the right-hand notes are played on ride cymbal **(both cymbals are reinforced with the bass drum)**. The unaccented notes remain on the snare, and the hi-hat is played on beat 2.

Example 10.25

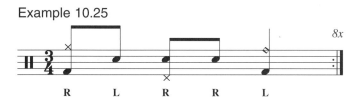

R   L   R   R   L

3. The Abbreviated Single Paradiddle—A Typical Four-Bar Phrase:

In this example, this rudiment is played around the kit in a typical four-bar phrase. The hi-hat is played on beat 2.

Example 10.26

R   L   R   R   L   R   L   R   R   L   R   L   R   R   L   R   L   R   R   L

Chapter 4: Trading Fours

In the following example, the drums trade fours through two choruses of a 32-bar ABAB form. The guitar (or other instrumentalist) begins the first chorus and drums follow afterward. For demonstration purposes, I have implemented the Flam Accent No. 1 (with tom accents) for letter A and the Single Drag (on the snare) for letter B.

Example 10.27

Track 70

Chapter 5: The Chart and Play-Along

Track 71 Demo
Track 72 Play-Along

Example 10.28

Form:

1. **Head:** A "broken three" feel
2. **1 Chorus** of Guitar Solo in a walking "three" feel. Per Unit 1, you must switch ride surfaces for each section.
3. **1 Chorus** of trading fours in a walking "three" feel. The guitar starts the trading.
4. **Head:** Return to the "broken three" feel
5. **Outro/Ending:** Tag the last two bars of letter B 3 additional times (4 times total) to form a definitive ending.

Unit Eleven: Brush Patterns

Scan for bio.

Jack DeJohnette

Description

In this unit, you will learn to play two medium tempo brush patterns and use them within an AABA form.

Upon completion of this unit, you should be able to:
- Play the "conventional stroke" brush pattern within a two-feel
- Play the "eyes" brush pattern within a walking feel
- Use both patterns within this unit's AABA tune

Chapter 1: Brush Background and Basics

In the late 1800s, many New Orleans drummers were looking for ways to create new, interesting, and softer sounds on the drumset. Therefore, they used fly swatters to caress and "trill" rhythms on a calfskin snare drum head. Soon thereafter, Julian F. Bigelow of Worchester, Massachusetts invented the first wire fly swatter, which became the first drum brush. It retailed for 15 cents and looked like this:

Example 11.1

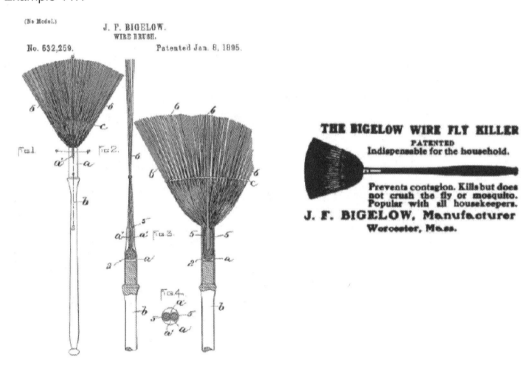

In 1901, the Louis Allis Company invented a retractable fly swatter brush (example 3.2). The Allis fly killer was granted a patent in 1913, and theirs was the design that Ludwig & Ludwig copied when they released their "Jazz Sticks" in the 1920s. Any differences between these two company's products were mainly cosmetic. By 1928, Ludwig & Ludwig created a retractable model for their Jazz Sticks. Later, Allis & Wiens followed Ludwig's lead by marketing their product as a "drumbeater" (in addition to selling it as a conventional fly swatter).

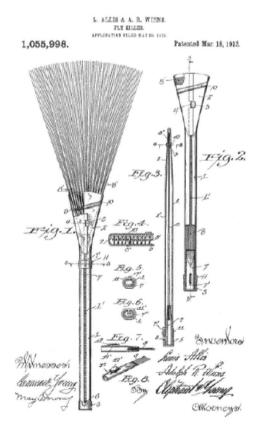

Example 11.2

Sound

Brushes produce a legato (long), warm, and smooth-flowing sound at all tempos and low volume levels. When played correctly, brushes mimic the sound of the ocean—a sustained "sshhhhhhhhh." Good brush playing requires many of the same skills as playing with sticks: a good touch and sound, supporting the soloist (comping), and an overall solid timekeeping feel.

Traditional Grip with a Sustained Motion

In order to achieve a pleasing sound with brushes, the left hand must make circular motions across the snare head "in-time." This is accomplished by using the tips of the brushes to gently sweep the brush over (and across) the drumhead rather than pushing downward with the body of the brush into the drumhead. A "traditional grip" makes this playing angle and stroke a bit easier to execute (even if you do not normally play this grip).

Example 11.3

Right Hand

While the left hand is playing a raised position and sustained motion, the right hand utilizes a matched grip on the snare drum (below). Depending on the type of stroke, this hand can be either level with or raised above the drum.

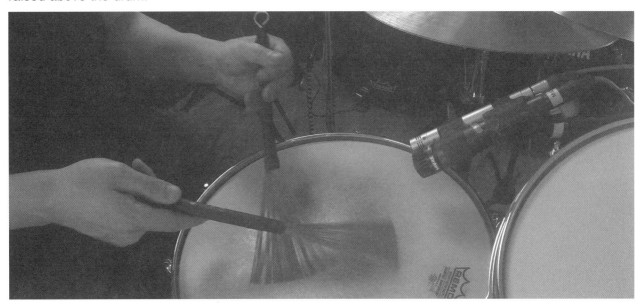

Example 11.4

Chapter 2: Brush Patterns

Key: Basic Motions

All brush strokes begin at the starting point, which is labeled with a tail arrow. These initial strokes move toward the point of the arrow. The distance between the tail and the point serves as a pick-up. The strokes **labeled as L.H.** are played with the left hand and the strokes **labeled R.H.** are played with the right hand.

The **thin lined** broken arrow is to be played **off the drum**. Most brush diagrams indicate the arrow point as beats 1 and 3 and the arrow tail as beats 2 and 4, but some diagrams will indicate the arrow point as all four beats (quarter notes). This indicates that a complete circle will be required for each beat.

Example 11.5

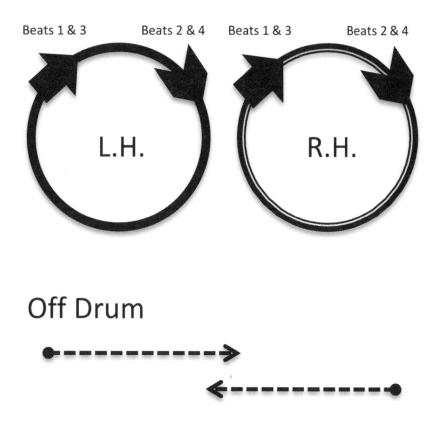

Two Main Patterns

In this unit's chart, we are going to use two popular brush patterns: (1) the conventional stroke and (2) big eyes. Let's take a look at each in detail.

The Conventional Stroke

The conventional stroke has the same rhythmic structure as the conventional jazz ride cymbal pattern. This brush pattern can be used for medium and uptempo jazz timekeeping.

The Right Hand

Begin at the tail of the arrow, using the broken triplet as your pick-up. Then move to the point (beat 1). Lift and return to the tail (beat 2). Repeat this pattern for beats 3 and 4.

The Left Hand

In a half note rhythm and a clockwise direction, circle continuously by starting at the tail and moving towards the point (the first beat). Complete this circle at the tail by gently swiping at the second beat.

Track 73

Example 11.6

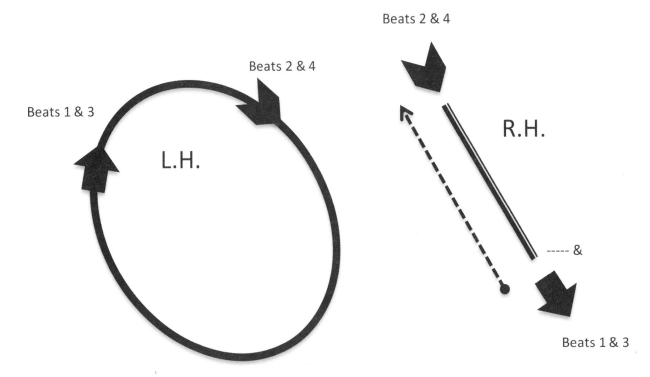

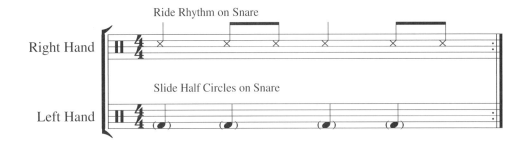

Big Eyes

This brush pattern has a quarter-note pulse, which can be used for slow, medium, and uptempo jazz timekeeping.

The Right and Left Hands

Both hands start at the tail at the center of the drum and make complete circles for each quarter-note beat. The right hand should move clockwise and the left hand should move counterclockwise. Keep both hands even and crossing the arrow of each point simultaneously. For best results use the hand positions below:

Track 74

Example 11.7

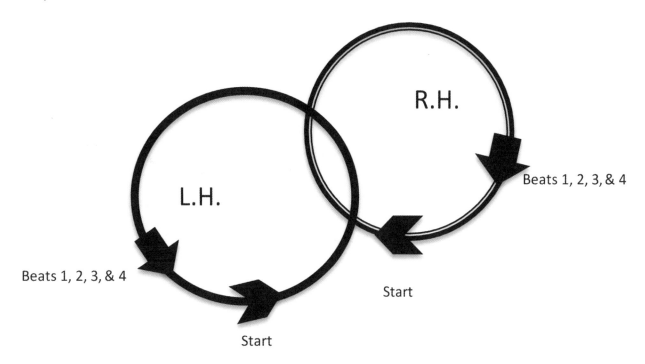

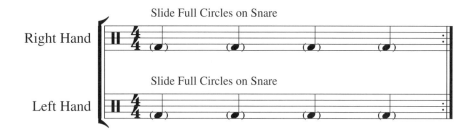

Chapter 3: Brush Patterns within an AABA

This unit's song is a 32-bar AABA lead sheet with two distinct feels: a two-feel for the A sections and a walking feel for the bridge:

Example 11.8

Brushes: The A Section

During the A section, you will play the conventional stroke as shown in example 11.6 alongside a two-feel (in the feet) like this:

Example 11.9

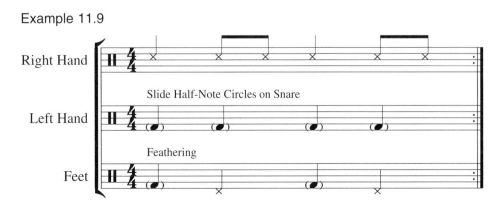

Brushes: The B Section

During the B section, you will play the Eyes pattern as shown in example 11.7 alongside a walking-feel (in the feet) like this:

Example 11.10

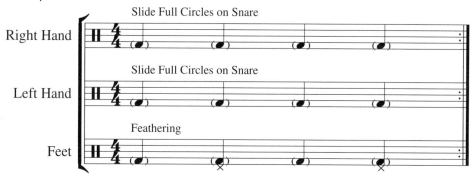

Choruses of Solo: Walking-Feel

During the solo sections, each pattern will be used for its respective section. However, each pattern will be used alongside a walking bass line and jazz foot pattern.

Chapter 4: The Chart and Play-Along

Track 75 Demo
Track 76 Play-Along

Example 11.11

Form:

1. **1 Chorus** of the Head: A: Two-Feel—Conventional Stroke. B: Walking-Feel—Eyes Pattern
2. **1 Chorus** of Guitar Solo—All walking-feel
3. **1 Head**
4. **Outro/Ending:** Tag the last two bars of letter A 3 additional times (4 times total) and end on the final bar (no. 25)

Unit Twelve: Brush Comping

12

Scan for bio.

Max Roach

Description

In this unit, you will learn to brush comp within the conventional stroke, trade fours, and play a full solo in the style of Max Roach. A new 32-bar tune will also be presented.

Upon completion of this unit, you should be able to:

- Play brush comping with timekeeping clichés
- Play the Triplet Swipe
- Play a Max Roach-style brush time feel
- Trade fours in the Max Roach brush style

Chapter 1: Conventional Stroke Brush Comping

In Unit 11 we learned to play brushes with traditional swing patterns. In this unit, we will learn to play comping variations within the conventional stroke. With this in mind, let's review this pattern:

The Conventional Stroke

As you saw in Unit 11, the conventional stroke has the same rhythmic structure as the jazz ride cymbal pattern and timekeeping feel. It can be used for medium and up-tempo jazz timekeeping. I have listed it below for your reference and review:

Example 12.1

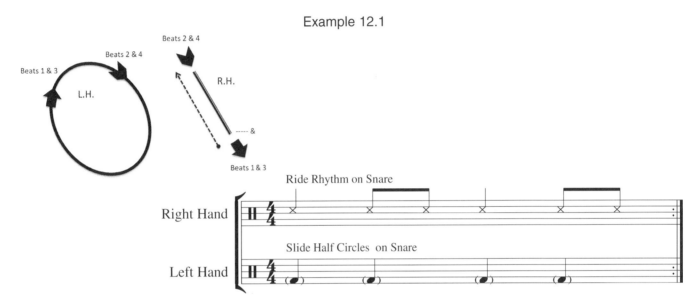

Comping within the Conventional Stroke

Generally speaking (and when using the conventional stroke), comping occurs with the left hand and hi-hat foot. Let's take a look at both in detail.

The Left Hand

Most of the accents that you will "comp" fall on the left hand and will require you to modify the half-note circular motion of the conventional stroke. Just like you "swipe" to mark beats 2 and 4, you will also use this "squeeze-swipe" in traditional grip to play each comping accent with your left hand. Your unaccented circular notes will be played in the normal position with the tip of the brush (example 12.2). Although to play accents within the conventional stroke's circular motion, you will dip your left hand and place the brush flat on the drumhead (example 12.3).

Example 12.2

Example 12.3

The Left Foot: Splashing the hi-hat to mimic a dedicated cymbal player

Oftentimes jazz drummers want to continue the legato sounds of the brushes, but on another voice (other than the snare drum). This usually occurs on the hi-hat with an open and splashing sound. This mimics the hand-held crash cymbals that were played by a dedicated cymbal player in a New Orleans Street Beat marching/funeral procession. Additionally (and depending on where you start your accent), each hi-hat note should remain open and ring into the next beat 2 (or 4). This technique is executed by hitting the heel-plate and foot pedal (of the hi-hat stand) in unison. Let's take a look at both steps:

With the hi-hat closed (and toes placed at the top of the stand), strike downward with your heel:

Example 12.4

Now, the hi-hats will splash-open and your foot will be flat on the footboard. However, your toes should remain off (above) the board slightly so they do not apply pressure and choke off the open hi-hat ring:

Example 12.5

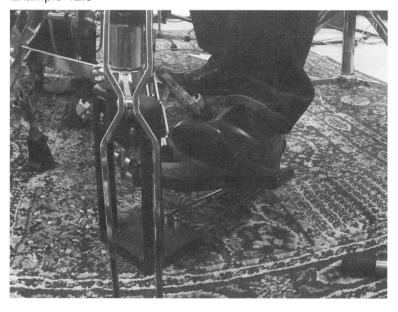

This is one technique to achieve this sound. However, there are many ways to accomplish this same result. For instance, many drummers play hi-hat splashes with their heel down while others prefer a rocking motion. Thus, feel free to experiment with your own adaptations of this technique.

Preliminary Comping Exercises for Hi-Hat

I have compiled some basic preliminary exercises that will help you to isolate each open hi-hat splash stroke alongside the feathered quarter-note bass drum pattern. Make sure to work through these exercises (before attempting to play the comping exercises on the following page).

Track 77

The Feet

Example 12.6

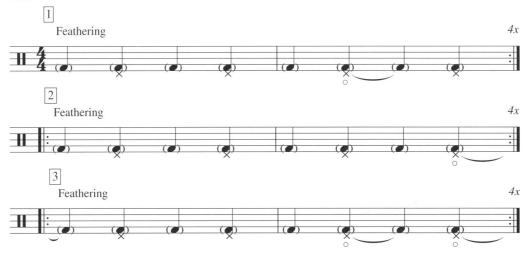

Adding the Conventional Stroke

I have compiled some basic preliminary exercises that will help you to isolate each open hi-hat splash stroke alongside the conventional stroke. Just as in the last set of examples, make sure to work through these exercises before attempting to play the comping exercises for both voices on the following page.

Track 78

Example 12.7

Preliminary Comping Exercises for Both Voices

Now that we have worked through examples 12.6 and 12.7, it is time to isolate each left-hand "swipe"—comping within both our conventional stroke and open hi-hat splash strokes. Not only will this help you gain the coordination required to perform these within this unit's tune, but it will also aid you in "internalizing" your Unit 12 brush patterns. Make sure to work through these exercises before attempting the chart.

Track 79
(Ex. 12.8-12.12)

Example 12.8*

Brush Comping Clichés within a Two-Bar Form

Once numbers 1–5 are comfortable, you should practice them within a two-bar cliché phrase like this:
(Notice that the hi-hat in the second measure splashes on beat 2 within the conventional stroke.)

Track 80
(Ex. 12.13-12.16)

Example 12.13

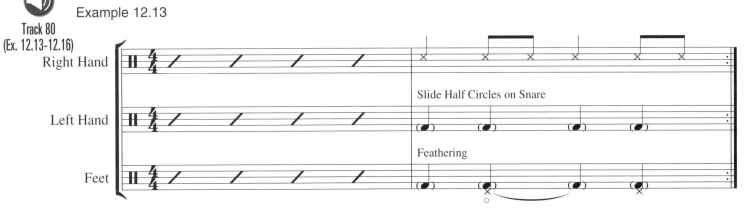

* Note: On the audio, example 12.8 precedes each rendition of the subsequent examples.

Therefore, if you inserted example 12.9, it would be played like this:

Example 12.14

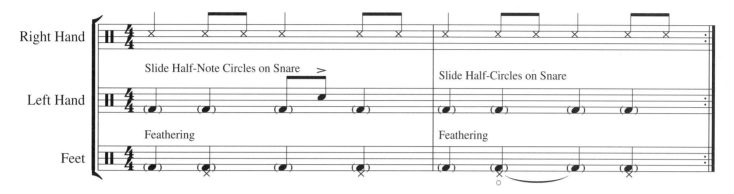

Brush Comping Clichés within a Four-Bar Form

Once numbers 1–5 and the two-bar comping clichés are comfortable, continue to practice them within a four-bar cliché phrase like this:

Example 12.15

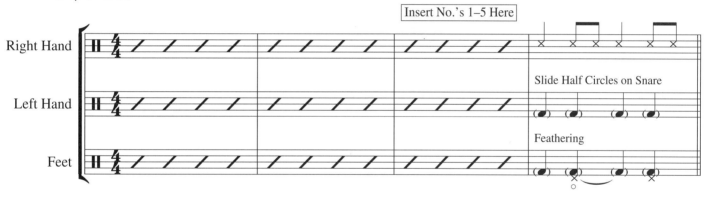

If you inserted Example 12.9 it would be played like this:

Example 12.16

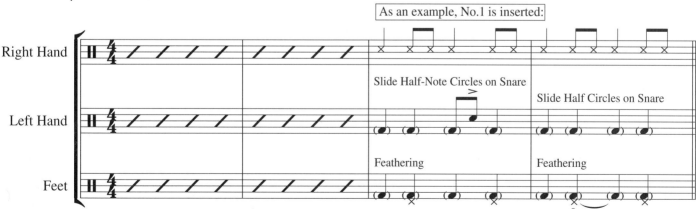

The Triplet Swipe

The Triplet Swipe is a specialized drum stroke used in both timekeeping and solo formats. The left hand pulls downward in the traditional grip, swiping quarter notes. The right hand taps the last two eighth-note triplets of each quarter-note subdivision.

Track 81
(Ex. 12.17-12.17b) Example 12.17

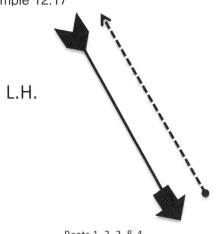

L.H.

Beats 1, 2, 3, & 4

The left-hand quarter notes "swipe."

R.H.

The right hand taps the last two eigth-note triplets.

Here is the pattern alongside our feathered bass drum and hi-hat 2 and 4 ostinato:

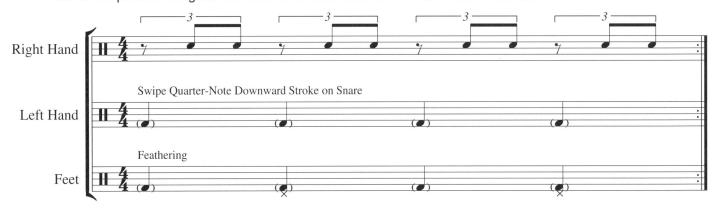

One-Handed Swipe

The One-Handed Swipe is a specialized drum stroke used in both timekeeping and solo formats. In this unit, we will use it in measures 13 and 14 of the Max Roach trading fours transcription from "Joy Spring." Let's take a look at how to execute this stroke in detail.

The right hand pulls from side to side, swiping sixteenth-note triplets.

Example 12.17b

Chapter 2: Bebop, Clifford Brown, and Max Roach

Created in the early 1940s, bebop differed drastically from the straightforward compositions of the swing era. While swing music tended to feature orchestrated big band arrangements, bebop music highlighted improvisation, fast tempos, asymmetrical phrasing, intricate melodies, and creative rhythm sections. The music itself seemed jarringly different to the ears of the public, who were used to the bouncy, organized, danceable tunes of Benny Goodman and Glenn Miller (i.e., the swing era). Instead, bebop appeared to sound racing, nervous, and often fragmented by long-winded improvised solos. Although, to jazz musicians and jazz music lovers, bebop was an exciting and beautiful revolution in the art of jazz. Two of the most famous musicians of the late late 1940s and early 1950s were trumpeter Clifford Brown and drummer Max Roach. Together, they formed the Clifford Brown and Max Roach Quintet.

Clifford Brown

Clifford Brown (October 30, 1930–June 26, 1956), aka "Brownie," was an influential and highly rated jazz trumpeter. He died at age 25, leaving behind four years' worth of classic recordings, most of which were with drummer Max Roach. Nonetheless, he had a considerable influence on later jazz trumpet players, including Donald Byrd, Lee Morgan, Booker Little, Freddie Hubbard, and Wynton Marsalis.

 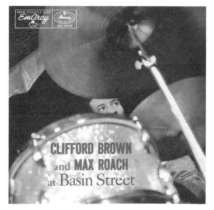 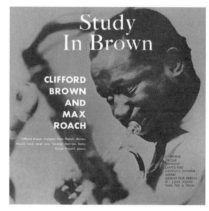

Clifford Brown and Max Roach Quintet

Clifford Brown and Max Roach is a 1955 album by the Clifford Brown and Max Roach Quintet. Not only was the album critically well received (and now a classic), but it also spawned two notable jazz standards: "Daahoud" and "Joy Spring." In addition, this record is also known for its textbook use of popular (now standard) forms such as AABA, ABAB, and 12-bar blues. Max's great improvised drum solos were also quite famous, as they built drum-based themes and melodies. This was a new approach to a jazz band's drum chair.

Chapter 3: Max Roach and Trading Fours with Brushes

In the previous chapter, we learned about bebop and Clifford Brown. We are now going to discuss Max Roach's drumming and his trading fours solo brush approach within this style and the song "Joy Spring" from the *Clifford Brown and Max Roach Quintet* album.

Background and Style

A pioneer of bebop, Max Roach is generally considered one the most important and influential drummers in history. He worked with many famous jazz musicians, including Coleman Hawkins, Dizzy Gillespie, Charlie Parker, Miles Davis, Duke Ellington, Charles Mingus, Sonny Rollins, and Clifford Brown. He recorded on the influential Miles *Birth of the Cool* record and went on to lead bands alongside Clifford Brown and as a leader in his own right.

Roach's most significant innovations came in the 1940s, when he and jazz drummer Kenny Clarke devised a new concept of musical time. By playing the beat-by-beat pulse of standard 4/4 time on the ride cymbal instead of on the swing-thudding bass drum, they developed a flexible, flowing rhythmic pattern that allowed soloists to play (and improvise) freely. This new approach also left space for the drummer to insert dramatic accents (also known as dropping bombs) on the snare drum, cymbals, and bass drum.

By "dropping bombs"—matching his rhythmic attack with a tune's melody—Roach also brought a new-found subtlety of expression to the drumset. He often shifted the dynamic emphasis from one part of his drumkit to another within a single phrase, creating a sense of tonal color and rhythmic surprise. The idea was to shatter musical conventions and take full advantage of the drummer's unique position. "In no other society," Roach once observed, "do they have one person play with all four limbs."

While this comping approach is common today, when Clarke and Roach introduced the new style in the 1940s it was a revolutionary musical advance. "When Max Roach's first records with Charlie Parker were released by Savoy in 1945," jazz historian Burt Korall wrote in the *Oxford Companion to Jazz*, "drummers experienced awe and puzzlement and even fear." One of those awed drummers, Stan Levey, summed up Roach's importance: "I came to realize that, because of him, drumming no longer was just time, it was music."

Let's take a look at Max's trading fours solo approach within "Joy Spring."

Trading Brush Fours from "Joy Spring"

"Joy Spring" is an AABA 32-bar tune, and Max trades fours for a chorus and also takes a full 32-bar solo thereafter. In this unit, we will concentrate on the first chorus of "fours" (and utilize them within our new tune, example 12.19, "Gordy Fall." Here are some performance notes:

1. Each "four" is played with brushes.
2. The hi-hat should remain on beats 2 and 4 throughout.
3. In bars 13–16, feather the bass drum on quarter notes.
4. In bars 21–24 and 29–31, continue to play the ride cymbal pattern with your right hand (within the conventional stroke).

Track 82

Example 12.18

Chapter 4: The Chart and Play-Along

This unit's tune is in the style of Clifford Brown and Max Roach's famous *Quintet* album. This AABA tune employs the conventional stroke brush timekeeping pattern within a walking-feel. Prior to the last head, we will also perform one chorus of trading fours per example 12.18.

Gordy Fall

Track 83 Demo
Track 84 Play-Along

Example 12.19

Form:

1. **1 Chorus** of the Head: Brushes—conventional stroke with comping patterns
2. **Chorus** of trading fours. Guitar starts and drums play each "four" as written within the solo transcription example 12.18
3. **1 Chorus** of the Head
4. **Outro/Ending:** Tag the turnaround (bars 21-24/the last four bars) 2 additional times (3 times total) to form a definitive ending.

Unit Thirteen: Max Roach Brush Solo

Scan for bio.

Gregory Hutchinson

Description

In this unit, you will learn to play a full 32-bar brush solo in the style of Max Roach.

Upon completion of this unit, you should be able to:

- Play a full 32-bar Max Roach brush solo
- Play two choruses of an AABA brush solo: (1) Trading fours with the Unit 12 solo and (2) a Max Roach full 32-bar solo

Chapter 1: Overview and Preliminary Analysis Exercises

In unit 12 we mastered many conventional stroke comping variations alongside trading fours within the Max Roach style. On the following pages, we will use these new skills together with a full AABA 32-bar Max Roach style brush solo. Let's break down this new solo into manageable four-bar fragments.

Preliminary Fragments for the "Joy Spring" 32-Bar Solo

In order for you to play the entire 32-bar "Joy Spring" type solo correctly and comfortably, I have listed many four-bar fragments to practice below. Although not notated, the hi-hat foot should close on beats 2 and 4. The stickings are included for your reference as well.

Bars 1-4 (Measures 33–36)

In the opening four bars, Max plays a syncopated eighth-note pattern into continuous hand-to-hand triplets, with each accent falling on the right hand.

Track 85
(Ex. 13.1-13.4)

Example 13.1

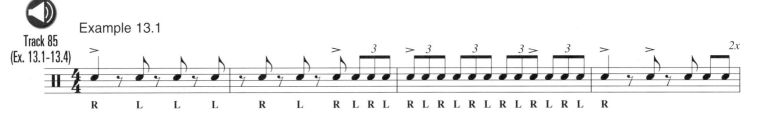

Bars 5–8 (measures 37–40)

In bar 37 (bar 5 of the solo), Max deviates from the standard 2 and 4 hi-hat pattern. The subsequent quarter-note triplet flam groupings between the snare and toms (and the snare flams themselves) should be played very "open," i.e., not in perfect unison.

Example 13.2

Bars 9–12 (measures 41–44)

Max returns to the alternating triplet phrases à la bars 1–4. Again, these triplet groupings are played hand-to-hand, with every snare and tom accent falling on the right hand.

Example 13.3

Bars 13–17 (measures 45–48)

In this example, Max continues his syncopated eighth-note phrasing alongside the previously mentioned alternating triplet motif.

Example 13.4

Bars 18–20 (measures 49–52)

During the bridge, Max continues to play hand-to-hand triplets, with every tom accent falling on the right hand. This is noted by the text: All Single Strokes. Each unaccented note should be played at *mezzo-forte*.

Track 86
(Ex. 13.5-13.8)

Example 13.5

L R L R L L R L R L R L

Bars 21–24 (measures 53–56)

Bar 53 continues the alternating triplets motif from the previous phrase, which transitions into two measures of straight sixteenth-note alternating strokes. The bridge (and phrase) concludes with swung, off-beat eighth notes à la the opening phrase.

Example 13.6

R L R L R L R L R L   R L R

Bars 25–28 (measures 57–60)

As Max returns to the last A section, his solo phrases become more rhythmically dense, as both the hands and feet are incorporated into the solo phrasing. Although beat 3 of the last bar (measure 60) is notated as an eighth rest and a subsequent eighth note, Max does not play a swung eighth note or a perfectly straight eighth note on this beat. It is more of a "rushed" eighth note. Therefore, I have placed this note within a box (for emphasis):

Example 13.7

R L R L   R

Bars 29–32 (measures 61–64)

This section continues the syncopated motif from the last phrase. Again, Max does not play a swung eighth note or perfectly straight eighth note on the highlighted beats below. It is more of a "rushed" eighth note. Therefore (and just as in the last example), I placed this note within a box (for emphasis). Notice the full measure of rest on bar 32 (measure 64).

Example 13.8

Bar 32 (measure 64)

Note: the last bar of the 32-bar chorus (measure 64) contains a whole rest. Thus, bar 64 is left empty in order to leave space for the two-beat melodic pickup and subsequent return to the head:

Example 13.9

Full Solo

Once you understand and have isolated each fragment, you should begin to prepare the fully notated solo. Performance notes: (1) This solo is played with the brushes, and (2) the hi-hat should remain on beats 2 and 4 throughout.

Example 13.10

Track 87

Chapter 2: Two Choruses of Solo

Now that you understand and can perform the full 32-bar solo, let's prepare Unit 12's full chorus of trading fours alongside example 13.10's full 32-bar solo. Therefore, you will be playing a full two choruses of solo for a total of 64 bars.

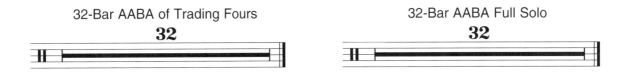

32-Bar AABA of Trading Fours   32-Bar AABA Full Solo

Trading Fours Review

For your convenience, I have reprinted a trading fours section here:

Example 13.11

Into the full solo:

Example 13.12

Chapter 3: The Chart and Play-Along

Track 88 Demo
Track 89 Play-Along

Example 13.13

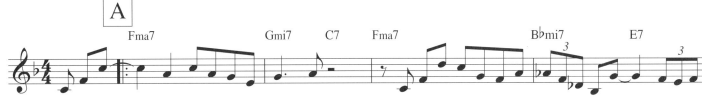

Form:

1. **1 Chorus** of the Head: Brushes—Conventional stroke with comping patterns
2. **Chorus** of trading fours. Guitar starts and drums play each "four" as written.
3. **1 Chorus** of drum solo. Play as written.
4. **1 Chorus** of the Head
5. **Outro/Ending:** Tag the turnaround (bars 22-25/the last four bars) 2 additional times (3 times total) to form a definitive ending.

Unit Fourteen: Jazz Mambo

Scan for bio.

Art Blakey

Description

In this unit, you will learn to play a mambo and jazz shuffle alongside an Afro-Cuban jazz tune. A 32-bar Art Blakey drum solo will also be presented.

Upon completion of this unit, you should be able to:
- Play an Afro-Cuban jazz mambo
- Play a jazz shuffle
- Understand and be able to play Art Blakey solo fragments
- Play a fully notated Art Blakey 32-bar drum solo

Chapter 1: Background – Afro-Cuban Jazz

In the 1940s, trumpeter Dizzy Gillespie was involved in a movement called Afro-Cuban jazz, which brought Afro-Latin American music and its rhythmic elements to a jazz, salsa, and pop audience. These rhythms included (but are not limited to) the mambo, guaguanco, and cascara. This style was considered bebop-oriented and some musicians of the day classified it as a modern movement. Afro-Cuban jazz was successful because it encouraged people to dance to its unique rhythms within a jazz concert (which was usually only a listening context). Gillespie's most famous contributions to Afro-Cuban music are the compositions "Manteca" and "A Night in Tunisia." As such (and in this unit), we will perform a tune in the style of these two famous compositions titled "A Day in Topanga."

A Night in Tunisia

"A Night in Tunisia" is a jazz standard written by Dizzy Gillespie. This was one of his staple tunes performed by both his big band and small group. Other artists have also heavily covered the song. As of 2009, the song appears as the title track of 30 CDs and is included in over 500 currently available CDs. In January 2004, The Recording Academy added the Dizzy Gillespie and His Sextet's 1946 Victor recording of "A Night in Tunisia" to its Grammy Hall of Fame.

Analysis

"A Night in Tunisia" uses unique oscillating half-step-up/half-step-down chord changes that give the song a distinctive, mysterious feeling. The tune's bass avoids the standard walking bass pattern of straight quarter notes. Here is an example that utilizes many of the aforementioned concepts:

Example 14.1

Art Blakey: *A Night at Birdland Vol. 1*

One of "A Night in Tunisia's" most famous performances is by Art Blakey's Jazz Messengers, who often gave show-stopping performances of the tune by adding extra percussion (played by the horn section). On the album *A Night at Birdland Vol. 1*, Blakey introduces "A Night in Tunisia" with a mambo-based drum vamp and concludes it with an Afro-Cuban (mostly African) inspired drum solo. This classic album and tune has become a standard of the Afro-Cuban jazz movement. The record also enlists an all-star band, which consists of Clifford Brown (trumpet), Lou Donaldson (alto sax), Horace Silver (piano), and Leon Russell (bass).

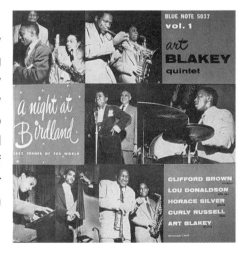

Chapter 2: The Mambo

Mambo is a Cuban musical rhythm, form, and dance style that achieved popularity in Havana, Mexico, and New York City. The word mambo means conversation with the gods in Kikongo, the language spoken by Central African slaves taken to Cuba.

In American jazz musical terms, the mambo refers to a bell pattern and several corresponding drumset patterns.

Mambo Bell

Track 90
(Ex. 14.2-14.6)

Example 14.2

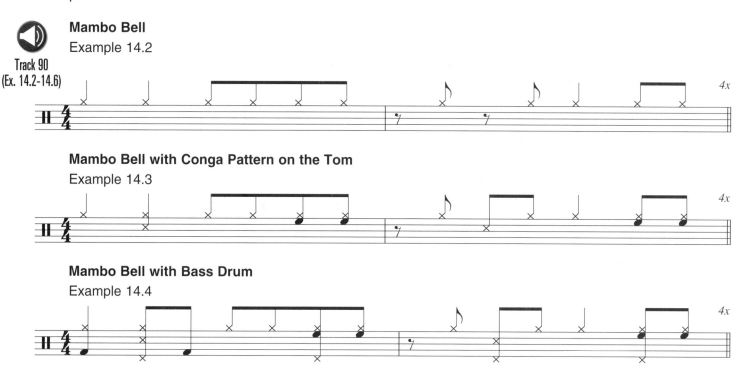

Mambo Bell with Conga Pattern on the Tom

Example 14.3

Mambo Bell with Bass Drum

Example 14.4

Mambo Bell with Bossa Nova Bass Drum

Many jazz drummers also fused the Afro-Cuban mambo pattern with a Brazilian bossa nova bass drum pattern. This is not a traditional pattern, but rather a homogenized version that is commonly used in a small group jazz context.

Example 14.5

Blakey Mambo

The Blakey mambo is a very unique jazz interpretation of the Afro-Cuban pattern, as it consists of swung (rather than straight) eighth notes. In addition, the cymbal bell is a modified version of the traditional bell pattern alongside a half-note bass drum pattern. The toms play on the "2&" and "4&" in a more African (than Cuban) manner.

Example 14.6 – Swung Eighths

Important Reminder: It is vital to realize that these patterns are not traditional Afro-Cuban patterns, but rather American jazz interpretations of these traditional rhythms.

Chapter 3: Art Blakey and a 32-Bar Solo

In the previous two chapters, we learned about Afro-Cuban jazz and the mambo. We are now going to discuss Art Blakey's drumming and his solo approach within this style and the song "A Night in Tunisia" from *A Night at Birdland Vol. 1*.

Background

Along with Max Roach and Philly Joe Jones, Art Blakey was one of the inventors of the modern bebop style of drumming. He is known as a powerful musician and a vital timekeeper; his brand of bluesy, funky grooving hard bop was and continues to be profoundly influential on mainstream jazz. For more than 30 years his band, Art Blakey and the Jazz Messengers, played (and wrote) many standards of the day such as "Moanin'," "Blues March," "Dat Dere," and "The Chess Players."

Style

Art's driving shuffle rhythms, his incessant 2-and-4 beat on the hi-hat, and consistent ride cymbal swing were readily identifiable. Unlike many drummers of his day, he was content to lay in the groove and provide the ultimate rhythmic (and oftentimes bluesy shuffle) timekeeping pad for each soloist. In 1948, Art visited Africa, where he studied polyrhythmic drumming. Soon thereafter, he began to incorporate the heavy use of syncopated toms within his timekeeping (and soloing) ideas.

The famous Blakey shuffle:

Example 14.7

Track 91

Notice that on beats 2 and 4 there is a dead stroke, which is when the stick is pushed into (and mutes) the drumhead.

Preliminary Solo Exercises for "A Night in Tunisia"

In order for you to play the entire 32-bar solo correctly and comfortably, I have listed many four-bar excerpts. Notice that stickings are included and that the hi-hat foot is notated (and closing) on beats 2 and 4. Again, this is an African-influenced solo. Thus, the snares should be turned off and the snare drum should be played as a tom sound.

Track 92
(Ex. 14.8-14.15)

Example 14.8

Example 14.9

Example 14.10

Example 14.11

Example 14.12. The 2 above the eighth notes indicates they should be performed as straight eighth notes.

Single Strokes...

Example 14.13. All sixteenth notes should be played straight.

RLRLR   RLRLR   Single Strokes...

Example 14.14. All sixteenth notes should be played straight.

Single Strokes...

Example 14.15. All sixteenth notes should be played straight. (The eighth notes are still swung.)

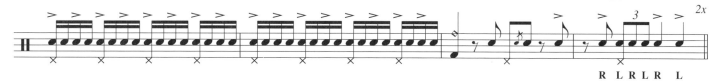

RLRLR L

The Full Solo from "A Night in Tunisia"

Once you have mastered each four-bar fragment, you can begin to build and perform the full 32-bar solo.
Please remember the performance notes from the preliminary exercises. After you have finished the solo,
practice returning to the Blakey (swung eighth note) mambo to reenter the head.

Example 14.16

Track 93

Chapter 4: The Chart and Play-Along

This unit's tune is in the style of Dizzy Gillespie's famous "A Night in Tunisia." This AABA tune employs the Blakey mambo during letter A and a walking swing feel during letter B. Prior to the last Head, we will also perform one chorus of a 32-bar Art Blakey drum solo transcription.

A Day in Topanga

Track 94 Demo
Track 95 Play-Along

Example 14.17

Form:

1. **1 Chorus** of the Head: Letter A—the Blakey (swung eighth) mambo. Letter B—Blakey shuffle.
2. **Chorus** of Guitar Solo: Both Sections—the Blakey shuffle (switching ride cymbals to mark the form)
3. **Chorus** of drum solo playing the written Art Blakey 32-bar solo with your hi-hat on beats 2 and 4
4. **1 Chorus** of the Head: Letter A—the Blakey (swung eighth) mambo. Letter B—Blakey shuffle.
5. **Outro/Ending:** Tag the last two bars of letter A 3 additional times (4 times total) to form a definitive ending.

Unit Fifteen: Ballad Brush Patterns

Scan for bio.

Kendrick Scott

Description

In this unit, you will learn to play two brush patterns and use them within a jazz ballad.

Upon completion of this unit, you should be able to:

- Utilize the "big eyes" brush pattern within a jazz ballad
- Play the "big eyes" pattern through a series of comping rhythms
- Play a jazz ballad brush pattern
- Play through a jazz ballad with both the "big eyes" and ballad brush patterns

Chapter 1: Using Eyes as a Ballad Pattern

For a jazz horn, piano, or string instrumentalist, playing a ballad allows for a great deal of lyrical expression and improvisation. It is the measuring stick for a performer's tone, worth, and overall mastery of his or her given instrument. Yet it is largely missing from a drummer's musical culture and is seldom addressed in learning situations. This unit will discuss two brush patterns and how to approach (and use them within) a jazz ballad.

Brush Ballad Sound

Again, brushes produce a legato (long), warm, and smooth-flowing sound at low volume levels. This is even more acute within a ballad. When a ballad is played correctly, the brushes mimic the sound of the ocean, i.e., a sustained "sshhhhhhhhhh." If this sound stops at any time, you have some work to do within your ballad playing!

Big Eyes

This quarter-note pattern is perfect for a ballad. It has wide circular motions, which can be stretched and elongated to fit the slow tempo of a ballad. While playing, this pattern's motion becomes much larger and it fills more (if not the entire) circumference of the drumhead.

The Right and Left Hands

To review from Unit 11's lesson, both hands start at the tail-center of the drumhead and make complete circles for each quarter-note beat. The right hand should move clockwise and the left hand should move counterclockwise. Keep both hands even and crossing the arrow of each point simultaneously. For best results use the hand positions here:

Example 15.1

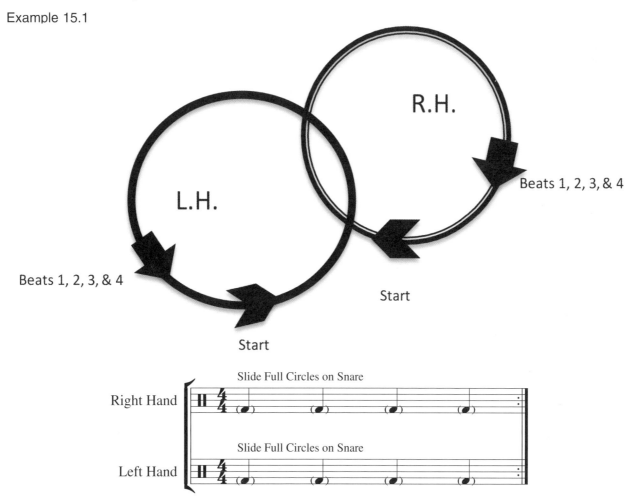

Additional Rhythms

Many ballads feature melodic elements that are stretched within the time. Therefore, a quarter-note rhythm (and eyes brush pattern) can get boring very quickly. With this in mind, I suggest that you amend this pattern to include both quarter-note triplet and straight eighth-note variations. The brush pattern and corresponding motions should remain unchanged. The following exercises (examples 15.2 and 15.3) will help you to vary your timekeeping approach while still staying out of the way of the instrumentalist's lyrical performance.

1. Quarter-Note Triplets

Using the big eyes motion, play through this quarter-note triplet rhythm:

Track 96
(Ex. 15.2-15.3) Example 15.2

2. Straight Eighth Notes

Afterward, and using the big eyes motion, play through this straight eighth-note rhythm:

Example 15.3

Three Practice Forms

Once you have mastered both patterns, please utilize them within small phrases. Bar one will be the traditional quarter-note big eyes pattern from Unit 12, and the other from the aforementioned variations used in examples 15.2 and 15.3. For example:

Track 97
(Ex. 15.4-15.6) Example 15.4

Example 15.5

Example 15.6

Further Practice

Once you have mastered each of the previous concepts, you should begin to improvise within the big eyes pattern. Here is one possible practice approach: play four bars of the quarter-note big eyes pattern, then play big eyes through various syncopated rhythms. I have listed two plausible options for you below:

Example 15.7

This technique can be employed alongside many classic texts, including Ted Reed's *Progressive Steps to Syncopation for the Modern Drummer* and Louis Bellon's *Modern Reading Text in 4/4*.

Chapter 2: Traditional Ballad Pattern

The traditional ballad pattern is very similar to the conventional stroke used within Unit 11, although some of these rhythmic elements are elongated to fill space and keep the legato sound swirling forward. Again, your motions should fill the entire circumference of the drumhead.

The Right Hand—Matched Grip

Without the brush touching the head, hold the brush at the starting arrow. Press down into the head on "ah" of beat 1 or 3. Then for beats 1 or 3, slide (and snap) into beats 2 or 4.

The Left Hand—Traditional Grip

Just as in the conventional stroke (and in a half-note rhythm and a clockwise direction), circle continuously by starting at the tail and moving towards the point (the first beat). Complete this circle at the tail by gently swiping at the second beat.

Track 98

Example 15.8

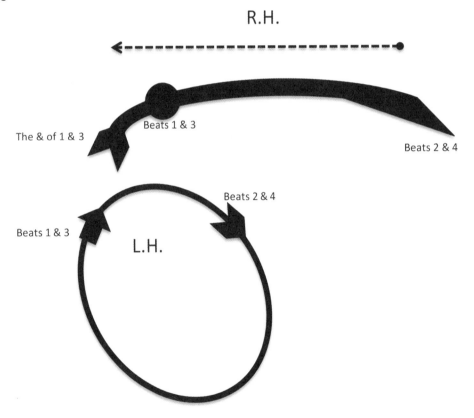

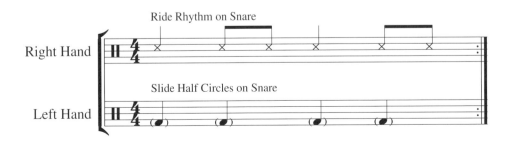

Chapter 3: Using Both Patterns within an ABAB

This unit's song has a 32-bar AABA form. Just as in our previously discussed Unit 5 AABA tune (played with sticks), you must clearly outline and mark both sections. Therefore, we are going to use the Big Eyes pattern for letter A and the traditional ballad pattern for letter B:

Example 15.9

Chapter 4: The Chart and Play-Along

Track 99 Demo
Track 100 Play-Along

Example 15.10

Form:

1. **1 Chorus** of the Head: A: Eyes Pattern B: Traditional Ballad Pattern
2. **1 Chorus** of Guitar Solo: A: Eyes Pattern B: Traditional Ballad Pattern
3. **1 Chorus** of the Head
4. **Outro/Ending:** Tag the last two bars of A 2 additional times (3 times total) to form a definitive ending.